CREATE

your own

WEBSITE

{ *using* **WORDPRESS** }

IN A WEEKEND

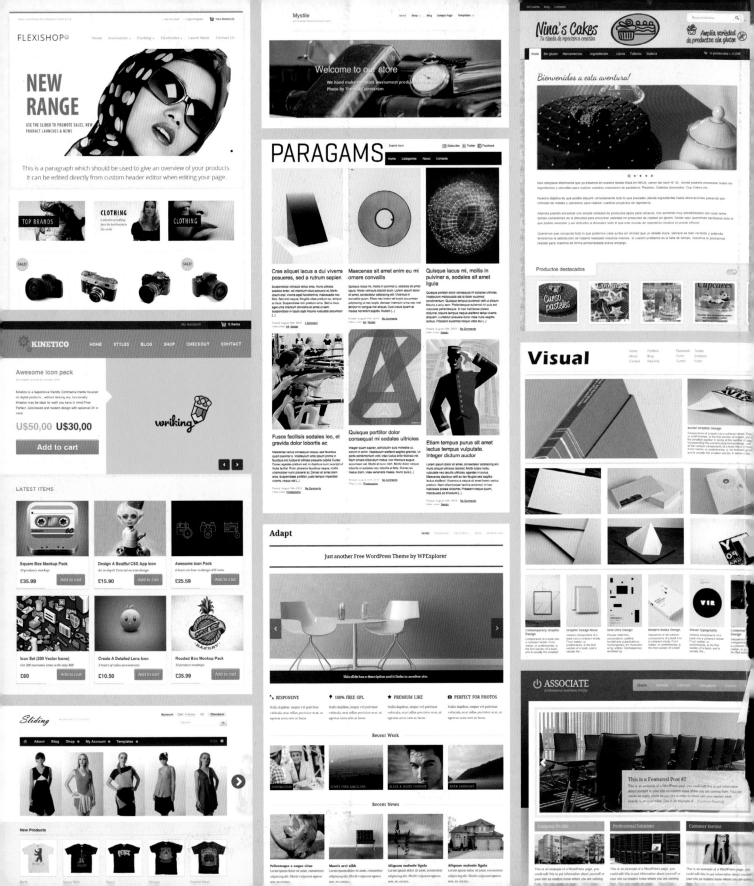

CREATE

your own

WEBSITE

{ *using* WORDPRESS }

IN A WEEKEND

ALANNAH MOORE

Focal Press
Taylor & Francis Group

NEW YORK AND LONDON

**CREATE YOUR OWN WEBSITE
USING WORDPRESS IN A WEEKEND**

First published in the USA 2013 by Focal Press
Focal Press is an imprint of the Taylor & Francis Group,
an informa business
70 Blanchard Road, Suite 402, Burlington, MA 01803, USA

This book was conceived, designed, and produced by
Ilex Press Limited, 210 High Street, Lewes, BN7 2NS, UK

Publisher: Alastair Campbell
Creative Director: James Hollywell
Managing Editor: Nick Jones
Senior Editor: Ellie Wilson
Commissioning Editor: Zara Larcombe
Art Director: Julie Weir
Designer: Simon Goggin
Color Origination: Ivy Press Reprographics

Library of Congress Cataloging in Publication Data:
A catalog record for this book is available from the
Library of Congress.

ISBN: 978-0-415-66268-0 (pbk)
ISBN: 978-0-203-38517-3 (ebk)

Printed and bound in China

10 9 8 7 6 5 4 3 2 1

TABLE *of*

CONTENTS

Why you need a website

AND WHAT THIS BOOK WILL DO FOR YOU

Today, every small business and many individuals need a website. Your website presents you or your business to the world. It is essential that it looks professional and that it presents you as you want to be seen, because it may well be your first and only chance to create the right impression.

Setting up a website doesn't have to be complicated, mystifying, or horribly expensive. In just a few hours, you can create something really professional that is exactly right for your needs—and you can do it all yourself, without having to pay for professional help.

You do not need to have any specialist knowledge to follow the steps in this book—it is written for people who are new to the world of website

building. Every reader will be able to complete their aim of getting their website set up online after just a few hours' work. If you are already computer-savvy, you'll find the book is full of pointers on how to develop your WordPress website at a more advanced level.

Thanks to WordPress, creating a wonderful-looking website is within everybody's reach. Whether you are a writer, an artist, an architect, or a gardener, whether you want to sell your products online or simply air your views, you'll find it easy to get yourself up and running online.

And you may even find you enjoy building your website so much that you'll want to dig in next weekend, too.

How this BOOK WORKS

AND WHAT YOU WILL NEED IN ADVANCE

This book functions a bit like a recipe book, with the recipes varying from simple to complex. First, we'll cover the basic "ingredients" you'll need before you can actually begin; then we'll go through all the elements you need to prepare a model website, which will act as the recipe or template for you to create a website using WordPress. Here you will learn all the background and techniques you'll need when you go on to tackle a more complex variation of the fundamental recipe.

For some readers, the basic template is all you'll need. The model website will make an excellent showcase for a small business. If you are happy with this perfectly functional and attractive-looking website, there may be no need for you to go further.

However, you will still need to read on, because you'll want to know some very important points concerning your website once it is live, like how to get people to visit it, and how to keep them coming back.

For those who want to embark on something more challenging, we'll also explore the creative possibilities of WordPress by looking at some more sophisticated website setups specifically designed for the different types of website you might want to create—e.g. business; art or photography portfolio; magazine/blog; or e-commerce (online store).

We'll also go into additional optional extras, such as how to accept payment from your website, how to extend the functionality that WordPress offers, and how to tie the whole thing in with social media.

So, it's up to you how far you want to go in your website-building adventure.

BEFORE YOU START

To set up your website over a weekend, you'll need to prepare the following in advance.

> Register your domain name and set up your website hosting (as explained in Chapter 2). Several hours are sometimes needed to point your domain name to your hosting, and some hosting packages require telephone validation.

> If you want to accept payment online using PayPal (see Chapter 6), you'll need to get your PayPal account set up and verified in advance.

> Do you need to get professional photographs taken (for example, of products you'll be selling)? If so, you'll need to arrange this and have the images to hand.

> Do you need to create a logo for your business to display on your website? You'll also need to have this ready to put on the site (see page 50).

> Read through the "Legal Issues" section on page 146, and carry out a trademark check if necessary. Make sure you have any other permits you may need.

COMPANION WEBSITE:
http://www.createyourwebsiteinaweekend.com, where you can check for updates and see working installations of WordPress websites.

1

An introduction to WordPress

WHAT IS WORDPRESS?

WordPress is a web-based system that can be used for free by anyone to build a website—all you need to do is install it on your web host, which usually takes just a few clicks, wait for a confirmation email, and away you go.

That's where the fun begins. WordPress is highly customizable, and there are thousands of beautiful templates (called "themes") available to choose from to create the look you want. Many of these are free, but even the "premium" themes (that you have to pay for) are surprisingly inexpensive.

WordPress was originally created as a blogging tool, but it has widened its reach vastly over the past few years, and is now used to create all kinds of websites. It is the most widely used content management system (CMS)—which is simply a system that allows you, the website owner, to easily log in, publish, and make changes through your internet browser (Internet Explorer, Safari, or whatever it is you use), without having to know anything about programming or coding. It is ideal for people who are setting up small businesses and don't want to spend a lot of money working with a web designer in order to get online. And of course, if you set the whole thing up yourself, you can update the site as often as you want to.

There are two versions of WordPress you can use. The simplest method is to set up a website that is hosted for you at WordPress.com. This is an excellent way to get up and running quickly; however it does have its limitations (as outlined on page 10). The "full" version of WordPress requires you to have your own domain name and your own hosting, but it offers you many more possibilities.

The full version is what we will be concentrating on in this book.

What makes WORDPRESS A GOOD CHOICE?

WORDPRESS GIVES YOU CONTROL OVER YOUR SITE

You don't have to be dependent on a webmaster to create or maintain your site. You have complete control.

IT'S EASY TO USE

It's easy to update your website, even if you're not particularly computer-savvy.

IT'S FLEXIBLE

WordPress can be used to create websites of all kinds: business sites, blogs, portfolios, magazine sites, e-commerce sites—you name it, WordPress can do it.

IT OFFERS THEMES

There are thousands of beautifully designed, full-featured, high-quality themes you can choose from, so you're bound to find a look that's just right for you. It's also very easy to change themes further down the line if you need to.

IT'S ROBUST AND SECURE

Any security holes are fixed with frequent updates to the system.

IT HAS A READY-MADE SUPPORT COMMUNITY

Because so many people use it, there is a huge support network to fall back on if you ever need any help.

> WordPress is the most used CMS in the world. There are over 58 million sites using WordPress.

Help is always at hand for WordPress users.

WordPress is used all over the world, and in over 120 languages.

WORDPRESS.COM *or* WORDPRESS.ORG?

So that you can choose which version of WordPress is right for you, we're going to look at some of the advantages and the downsides of each. Before looking at the tables, read through the descriptions to clarify the differences between the two.

WordPress.com is the version of WordPress that is hosted for you.

WordPress.org is the version of WordPress that you install on your own host, also known as "self-hosted" WordPress. It's referred to as "WordPress.org" because that's the central website you go to in order to download the software. (It's likely you won't actually have to do this, though, since most hosting companies have an easy-install system that enables you to install it with just a click or two directly from their control panel—we'll go through this later.)

HOSTED: WORDPRESS.COM
(For more on hosting see page 14)

PROS	CONS
It's very quick and easy to set up.	You have limited access to themes. WordPress.com offers you a good selection, but there are many, many more out there. You also don't have the option to upload a custom theme if you ever want to use one (a theme you've had especially designed).
You don't have to worry about any technical matters, such as security and backing up your site, as these are all taken care of for you.	You can't add plugins—extra components that add to the scope of your site.
You will get some website traffic just from being part of the WordPress.com community.	You can't tweak the code if you ever need to (or get anyone else to tweak it for you).
There is no concern about your site ever going down or being unavailable—but then again, if you are using a quality host, this should never be an issue.	You have limited storage space.
	They sometimes put ads on your site, and you have no control over this (unless you pay to remove them).
	You can't run your own ads on your site, should you want to.

COSTS
Free setup and hosting
Your own domain (mydomain.com instead of mysite.wordpress.com)—$13–$25/year
Optional paid-for themes—starting at $39 (once-only payment)
Optional "No-Ads" upgrade—$30/year
Other optional "upgrades" such as increasing your storage space—various prices
Switching to self-hosted at any point in the future (they'll do it for you; some hosting companies offer this service free when you switch over to them)—$129

SELF-HOSTED: WORDPRESS.ORG
(For more on hosting see page 14)

PROS	CONS
You can install whatever theme you like, free or premium, from a selection of thousands.	You have to handle the hosting yourself.
You can add plugins.	You are responsible for all the upgrades and backups yourself.
You can fiddle with the code if you need to (or get someone else to).	The WordPress interface is fairly simple, but you will have to acquire some technical knowledge.
No limit to the amount of storage space (you are only limited by the hosting package you choose).	
No ads (unless you want to run your own, which you are able to do if you choose).	

COSTS
Your own domain—around $10 a year (this may be included in your hosting package)
Hosting—depends on your host; at its lowest, approximately $30 a year, more usually around $100 a year
Optional paid-for theme—starting at $30 (a once-only payment)

In a nutshell, WordPress.com represents a great choice if a blog is what you need and you want to get up and running quickly. If you want to create anything more complex with your site, or may wish to do so in the future, it's best to dive into the self-hosted version from the outset.

Below left: WordPress.org—the home of the self-hosted version of the system.

Below: WordPress.com—sign up here to set up your hosted WordPress site.

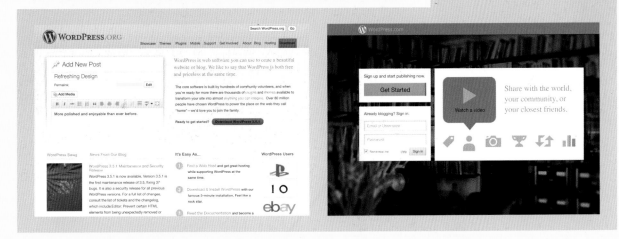

The elements of a **WORDPRESS WEBSITE**

Before you start planning your website, it makes sense to get familiar with the different elements of a site created using WordPress.

What does a WordPress website look like? The chances are that you have seen many WordPress websites without realizing it, because the thousands of different themes available make them all look quite different.

There are WordPress themes designed for all kinds of websites—see Chapter 7 for some examples of the range of designs available to choose from. Here, we see a theme designed as a business/creative portfolio. Many themes include separate layouts for the home page and the blog page; others also include additional layouts, such as the portfolio page layout you can see here.

Portfolio page layout.

1. **The logo.** Some sites alternatively have **header text** at the top and/or a **header image** that stretches the width of the site.
2. **The menu.**
3. **Page text.** Most business sites will choose to have introductory text on their home page, but with all WordPress sites, you can set it so that your blog or news posts appear here instead, if yours is a more blog-style or news-based site.
4. **Slider.** Many themes feature a rotating image slideshow, known as a slider, on the home page.
5. **The footer.** Most websites show a copyright notice in the footer; some themes also allow you to put widgets (see No. 9) in this area.
6. **The background.**
7. **Social media buttons.**
8. **The sidebar.**
9. **Widgets.** Elements inside the sidebar (for example, the titles of the latest blog or news posts) are called widgets.

The "Bigbang" theme by Brankic1979,
available from ThemeForest; home page layout.

Blog page layout.

2

Your domain and hosting

DECIDING ON A DOMAIN NAME AND A HOST

Before you start building your website, there are two things you need:
> a domain name
> hosting for your website

A domain is the web address of a website. For example, Google's domain name is www.google.com.

For a self-hosted WordPress site, you will need to buy a domain name. If you use WordPress.com, you will be given an address that looks something like this: mysite.wordpress.com. Or you can purchase your own domain and use it with your WordPress.com site. I recommend you do this if you're using the hosted version, as having a website with wordpress.com in it doesn't look very professional.

Domain names cost in the region of $10 a year, and they can be purchased from a company called a registrar (or, if you're using WordPress.com, you can purchase it through them at a cost of $18 [at time of writing]). Some hosting companies include the cost of your domain in their price, so depending on whom you choose for your host, you may not need to set the two up separately.

We'll look at some places to register your domain name on page 17.

The second thing you will need is hosting for your website. You can consider your hosting company as the "landlord" of the plot of ground in cyberspace on which you will construct your website.

It's essential that your hosting company is reliable—your website should never be "down" or unreachable, which can happen from time to time with less-reliable hosting companies.

We'll address how to choose a reliable host suitable for your needs shortly. First, there are some things you should bear in mind when choosing your domain name.

Choosing a DOMAIN NAME

You have three basic choices to make when choosing your domain name.

These are:
> your brand or business name
> a search-engine-friendly name
> a more creative name

Personally, I'd always go for the brand name, if it is available, over a search-engine-friendly name, as that's how people will remember you.

A domain name should be:
> easy to spell, and easy to pronounce (I'd avoid hyphens, as you'll need to spell it out on the telephone)
> not too long—keep it short, catchy, and memorable
> not too similar to your competition's domain name
> very definitely not a violation of someone else's trademark (see page 146).

WHICH EXTENSION SHOULD YOU USE—.COM, .NET, ETC.?

A .com domain name is almost always preferable. Choosing a .net or a .org domain may seem like a great solution if the .com domain you wanted is unavailable, but it will almost certainly result in confusion. The .com extension is so widely used that many people will assume your domain is a "dotcom," and you will most likely find yourself pointing out the different extension specifically each time you quote your domain

name . . . not to mention that you will also end up sending a stream of accidental traffic to the other .com website with the same name.

Having said that, although .com is usually preferable, there is an exception: if you are not based in the U.S., and you expect only to do business in your country of residence, the country-specific version of the domain name may be a better choice as it will indicate

straight away to visitors that your business is local. Until recently, the more unusual extensions such as .me were a no-no for serious business sites; today, they are more frequently used, which indicates that they are becoming more acceptable. The only time I would suggest using one, however, is if you can come up with a witty idea (see page 16) that makes good use of it, in which case it will be a positive asset to your business.

Your choices for the kind of domain you register are:
> the "classic" extensions of .com, .net, and .org
> a country-specific extension, such as .co.uk, .it, .ie, or .es, etc.
> more unusual extensions, such as .tv, .biz, .mobi, .me, .co, etc.

GETTING CREATIVE

It is true that many .com domains have been taken. But there are plenty more out there if you can use a bit of imagination. It's even better if you are starting your business from scratch now, as you can choose a brand name and a domain at the same time, and then come up with something truly unique and memorable.

CHECKING YOUR DOMAIN NAME

Googling a domain name isn't a reliable way of checking its availability. If there's nothing on a site, it doesn't mean that it is available—it might mean it just isn't in use. Use a registrar like namecheap.com instead for your research, or a tool such as www.instantdomainsearch.com.

TIP

To find out who owns a domain already registered, visit www.betterwhois.com.

Domainsbot.com

Try these tools to help you come up with domain name ideas:
http://www.instantdomainsearch.com
http://www.domainsbot.com

Namestation.com

http://www.namestation.com
http://www.nameboy.com
http://domai.nr
http://www.dotomator.com

Here are a few ways you can come up with original brand/domain names:
> put two words together to create compounds—YouTube, Firefox, Facebook
> use phrases—StumbleUpon, MySpace, SecondLife
> use slogans—justdoit.com (Nike), haveityourway.com (Burger King), powerofdreams.co.uk (Honda UK)
> combine parts of words—Microsoft, Farecast, Wikipedia

> misspell words—Flickr, Digg, Goowy
> change or add a letter to create variations on words—Zune, iPhone, iTunes
> add prefixes and suffixes—Friendster, Napster, Biznik
> invent words—Etsy, Odeo, Bebo
> use words from other languages—Rojo, Vox
> play around with unusual or country-specific extensions—del.icio.us, foot.ie, designm.ag

Registering a DOMAIN NAME

Before you register a domain name, you need to choose your host (see page 19)—if your hosting package includes a domain name, you can skip this section.

If you're choosing a country-specific domain name, check your hosting company can register it for you. It may be that you'll need to register it separately.

It's very important to choose a reputable domain-name registrar. Smaller companies can disappear, and you may find your precious domain name in the hands of someone completely different.

Therefore, it's best to go with one of the bigger names in the field—for example:

> www.namecheap.com
> www.godaddy.com
> www.gandi.net—which offers good prices for country-specific domains

If you're going to use WordPress.com, you'll register your domain directly through them. We'll see how this works on page 37 when we go through the setup of a WordPress.com blog.

Namecheap.com and Godaddy.com—two reliable domain registrars.

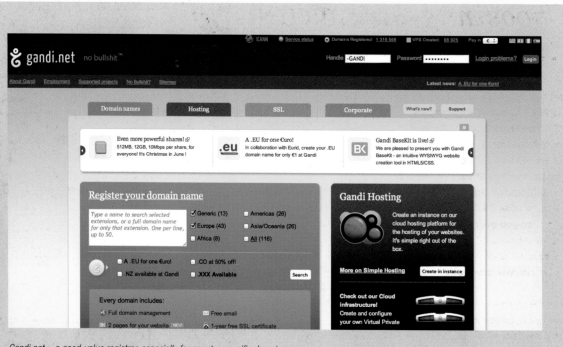

Gandi.net—a good-value registrar, especially for country-specific domain names.

TIP

Make sure you sign up for your domain with an email address you use regularly. You will only receive reminders for renewal via this email address. It is also a good idea to set a calendar reminder for a week or so before the date, just in case you miss the emails. You really don't want to lose your domain.

BUYING OTHER EXTENSIONS

In addition to the .com, you may also want to buy .net, .org, or any other applicable country-specific version of your domain to prevent anyone else getting hold of them. You may want to snap up the hyphenated version of your domain name as well, if applicable.

DOMAIN AND HOSTING PACKAGES

When registering your domain, it is likely you will be offered hosting by the registrar, and possibly other services at the same time, such as email. My advice is to ignore these offers and head to one of the dedicated hosting companies, such as those recommended on the next page.

Choosing your HOSTING

You need to choose a web host that has the following capabilities.

> It must be capable of running PHP and MySQL (in order to run WordPress).
> It should feature a one-click install for WordPress (to make the installation as simple as possible).
> It must offer 24/7 technical support (in case you ever have any issues).
> It must have a superb uptime record of 99–100 percent (meaning your site will never be unavailable).

Your business—or your website—may grow, or you may want to build other websites.

If that's a possibility, you'll want to find a package that also includes:

> unlimited storage (so your site can grow as big as it needs to)
> unlimited bandwidth (so you can accommodate a stampede of visitors)
> unlimited databases (allowing you to create additional WordPress sites if you want to)
> the possibility of hosting unlimited domains
> an unlimited number of email addresses.

For most small-business needs, "shared" hosting is perfectly adequate. This merely means sharing a server's services with other customers (who you'll never be aware of). If you ever need anything more sophisticated, it is a simple matter to upgrade to a virtual private server or dedicated hosting.

We won't go into the precise details of the different kinds of hosting here, as "shared" hosting is probably all you'll ever need; however, if you do need more information, you can refer to the hosting companies' websites.

Here are some recommended hosting companies:
DreamHost*
http://www.dreamhost.com
Bluehost
http://www.bluehost.com
MediaTemple
http://mediatemple.net
HostGator
http://www.hostgator.com
Webhostingpad
http://www.webhostingpad.com
(the cheapest I have come across)

*DreamHost is my favorite due to their superb uptime record and good customer service. Its shared hosting package has all of the extra features I've listed to look out for.

ONE-CLICK INSTALL
It's essential you choose a web host that offers a one-click install. The manual procedure is simple for someone more experienced, but for a beginner, it's an unnecessary headache you really don't want for your weekend website setup.

DreamHost—my personal recommendation due to their superb uptime record and good customer service.

Webhostingpad.com—the least expensive host found thus far.

Linking your DOMAIN AND HOSTING

If you've chosen a hosting package that includes a domain name, you'll be able to skip this section. However, if your hosting company requires you to register a separate domain name, or if you have purchased a country-specific domain that your hosting company can't supply you with, you will need to register your domain and sign up with a hosting company separately, and then link the two.

Once that's done, when your site visitors type your website address into their internet browser, they'll be able to see whatever web page has been uploaded onto your hosting space. For the moment, it will just be a holding page, as you haven't put anything onto your website yet.

Here we will go through the steps using Namecheap (domain registrar) and Dreamhost (hosting company) as examples. For other companies, the principle will be the same, although the layout of their websites will look different.

NS1.DREAMHOST.COM   66.33.206.206
NS2.DREAMHOST.COM   208.96.10.221
NS3.DREAMHOST.COM   66.33.216.216

General
- Change Contacts
- Transfer DNS to Webhost
- Switch To DNS System v1
- Registrar Lock
- Auto-Renew
- List Domain for Sale
- TypoScan
- Whois Business Listing

○ Use NameCheap Hosting DNS Servers
● Specify Custom DNS Servers (Your own DNS Servers)

1. NS1.DREAMHOST.COM *
2. NS2.DREAMHOST.COM *
3. NS3.DREAMHOST.COM
4.
5.

Add More Nameservers

Save Changes

1. **Log into your host.**

2. **In Dreamhost,** go to Manage Domains > Add New Domain. Type your domain into the empty field next to "Domain to host" (there's no need to touch anything else). Scroll down a little and click the blue button that says "Fully host this domain."

3. **Once you've clicked** the blue button, copy these lines from the website. Paste them into a text file on your computer to save them temporarily.

4. **Now,** log into your domain registrar's website.

5. **In Namecheap,** click on the domain name listed under "Your Domains." On the left-hand navigation, under "General," click on "Transfer DNS to Webhost."

6. **Make sure** the button next to "Specify Custom DNS Servers" is clicked. Paste in the three nameservers—the three rows of the left-hand column that you copied from Dreamhost—as shown opposite. (Other registrars may require the lists of numbers, which are called IP addresses, but in this case, you are not asked for them.)

7. **Finally, click** "Save Changes," and you're done.

You'll know when your domain is successfully linked to your hosting company, because when you visit your website, you'll be able to see your host's holding page. This may happen almost instantaneously, or it may take a few hours.

HOW TO POINT A DOMAIN TO A WEBSITE

If you have purchased additional domains—for example, a hyphenated version of your domain name—in order to secure it, you will want to point it to the domain that will be your main website. (You can skip this section if it doesn't apply to you.)

For example, if you have bought my-domain.com and you want anyone who visits my-domain.com to immediately be transferred to your main website at mydomain.com, you will need to point my-domain.com to mydomain.com.

Here's how to do it, using Namecheap as an example. (For other registrars, the principle will be similar, but the website won't look the same.)

1. **Log into Namecheap.**

2. **Go to** My Account > Manage Domains. Click on the domain name you want to point to your main website.

3. **On the left-hand navigation**, find "All Host Records," and click on it.

4. **Configure** the top two rows on the page exactly as below, using your domain instead of "http://www.mydomain.com"

5. **Scroll down** the page and click the blue "Save Changes" button. The change should take effect within minutes.

HOST NAME	IP ADDRESS /URL	RECORD TYPE	MX PREF	TTL
@	http://www.mydomain	URL Redirect	n/a	1800
www	http://www.mydomain	URL Redirect	n/a	1800

3

Planning your website

YOU'VE GOT YOUR DOMAIN AND YOUR HOSTING SET UP. IT'S NOW TIME TO PLAN THE WEBSITE YOU'RE ABOUT TO BUILD.

What kind of site are you PLANNING TO BUILD?

A BUSINESS SITE (1)

You may need just a few pages to present your business and the services it provides, and perhaps additionally give some information about projects you've worked on or samples of previous work you've done. This kind of site is often referred to as a "brochure" site.

If this is the case, a simple website, such as the basic model site we will build together in Chapter 5, may be all you require. However, if you're planning to create something that looks slicker or has a more corporate feel, you'll want to look at the selection of business themes in "Exploring Themes" (Chapter 7), or use the chosen business theme we focus on in Chapter 8. Looking ahead and visiting other sites for comparison will help you clarify your ideas while you're at the initial planning stage.

A PORTFOLIO SITE (2)

Creatives, such as artists, designers, and photographers, will need to showcase their work online. There are dozens of beautiful themes designed to display portfolios—turn to page 96 to see some examples, and on page 109 we'll walk though the setup of such a site.

A MAGAZINE (OR BLOG) SITE (3)

This covers both personal blogs and news or magazine sites focused around a particular field of interest. Page 98 will give you a taster of some of the themes you can use, and on page 114, we will follow a step-by-step guide to the creation of a site using one of my favorite themes (pictured).

AN E-COMMERCE SITE (4)

Are you going to be selling from your site? There are quite a few options for doing this, which are discussed in Chapter 6 (page 82). It makes sense to decide now on which one you're going to implement—it may be that you want to choose a regular theme and just add payment buttons, or it may be that you want to kick off with a theme designed specifically as an online store. We'll look at the setup of one of these in detail on page 120.

Many websites will, of course, be hybrids—for example, a blog can be added to any kind of site, and business sites often contain a portfolio to showcase samples of work.

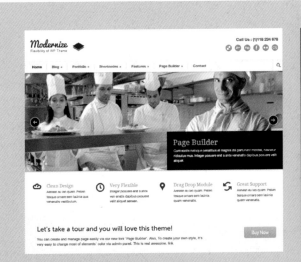

(1) "Modernize" by GoodLayers from ThemeForest.

(2) "Portfolium" by WP Shower.

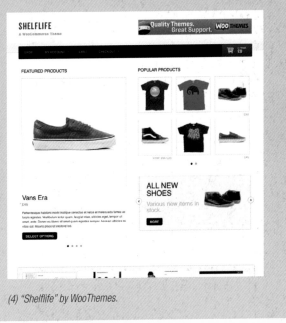

(3) "Structure Theme" by Organic Themes.

(4) "Shelflife" by WooThemes.

What's the purpose of **YOUR SITE?**

Every site has a purpose—usually more than one. Be clear on your purpose or purposes are before you start, as then you can make sure the layout and the content achieve these.

Common purposes are:
> to provide information
> to promote a service
> to sell products
> to build an email list of people to whom you can market your products in future
> to create a focal point for people who share the same interest
> to present yourself as an expert in your field

WHO IS YOUR TARGET AUDIENCE?

Who is going to be visiting your site? Is there a specific group of people, and are they young, old, innovative, conservative? It's essential to have a clear picture of your target audience, both when you are creating the content for your site and considering how you want it to look. Colors, style, writing tone, what visitors want to read about, or what they may need to know about you will all be determined by who your target audience is.

TIP

Pick a single particular person who fits the mold of the ideal visitor, and create your website with that person specifically in mind.

What's the difference between a blog and a website?
> A website is a general term for a location you visit on the internet.
> A blog can be part of a website, or it can act as a standalone.
> A blog can be more personal, and is more up-to-the-minute.
> A blog is a series of articles or pieces of news relating to somebody, a particular topic, or the activities or news of a business.
> Adding a blog to your website is one way of keeping your site dynamic; it also enables you to interact with your visitors. See page 134 for more reasons to include a blog on your site.

What content do you need on YOUR SITE?

For a basic business website, you will probably need to include the following pages (although you may choose to name them differently):

> Home
> About
> Services
> Products
> Testimonials
> Blog
> Contact

HOME

The "Home" page is what your website visitor will see first. Here you should let the visitor know clearly what it is you do and why they should be dealing with you.

The text should not be too lengthy, and you should remember it is your first—and possibly only—chance to impress and engage your visitor, as they are able to click away at any time.

Put yourself in your ideal visitor's shoes and imagine what you would like to see on your home page. What would convince you this was the right website to be on; that you had found the right people to deal with? Striking a decisive chord with your ideal customer is your primary aim.

Remember to check your spelling, grammar, and punctuation—it couldn't be easier with a spell-checker—and ask someone to proofread your copy. It's so easy to avoid messing up your first impression with glaring spelling or grammatical mistakes on your home page.

TIP

Look at your competitors' websites, or people doing the same thing as you. What content do they have on their sites? How do they organize their information? Take some time to surf around in your area of interest.

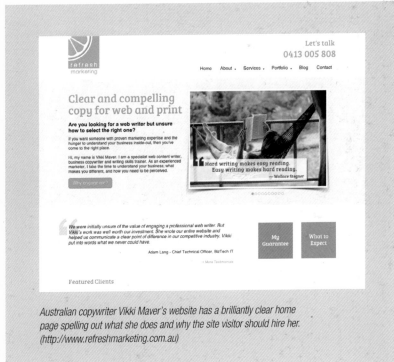

Australian copywriter Vikki Maver's website has a brilliantly clear home page spelling out what she does and why the site visitor should hire her. (http://www.refreshmarketing.com.au)

ABOUT

The "About" page provides more information about you or your business to visitors who want to know more.

It could include:

> the people involved in the business
> how long the business has been established
> the story behind the setting up of the business
> your personal/professional background
> the team
> photographs of you, or the team, or other photographs of interest
> perhaps a "human touch" or a bit of humor to remind the visitor there are real people behind the text on the page

SERVICES

I'm not overly keen on the title "Services" for a website, as it seems rather dry and uninviting—I prefer friendlier alternatives such as "Work With Us," but obviously those aren't always appropriate and "Services" may be your only real option.

Whatever you choose to call it, the "Services" area of your site needs to give details about what it is you do—the depth of detail is up to you. Do you want to encourage people to contact you to find out more, or do you want all the details to be provided on the web page? I don't recommend one strategy over the other; it may be useful to see how your competitors are presenting their services.

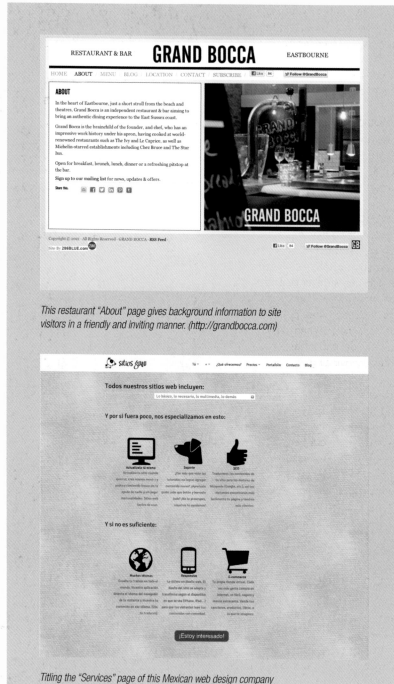

This restaurant "About" page gives background information to site visitors in a friendly and inviting manner. (http://grandbocca.com)

Titling the "Services" page of this Mexican web design company "Qué ofrecemos?" ("What do we offer?") sounds much more inviting than "Services." (http://sitiosguau.com)

Whether or not to include pricing details on your website is also an issue that only you can decide. If in doubt, you can test both options once your site goes live and see if there is a marked difference in results.

PRODUCTS

Similar to "Services," this page title can be very unengaging; an alternative such as "Our New Designs" might be more inviting.

TESTIMONIALS

There's nothing that impresses people more than testimonials from happy— better still, ecstatic—customers. If they are lukewarm, or don't convey enthusiasm simply because the person doesn't write particularly well, don't include them. Their job is to sell you, and it has to be 100 percent convincing.

If it makes you blush to display a page titled "Testimonials," you could just call it "Clients"—or include a small box at the bottom of your page entitled, "What clients have said," which will seem more discreet, but won't be overlooked. Some WordPress themes include a testimonials function that displays random testimonials on your page or in your sidebar.

BLOG

Whether you call it "Blog," or label it something different like "News" or "What's Happening," I can't think of a website that wouldn't be enriched by having a blog section built into it. Regularly updated, it is a great way to make your business look dynamic and bring projects you're working on to your visitors' attention (see page 134 for more).

Client testimonials appear at the bottom of the web pages for this Texan holiday cabin website; labeled "feedback," this is a nicely discreet way of integrating testimonials. (http://cabinsatsmithcreek.com)

CONTACT

It's common to include a web form on most websites so customers or readers can contact you easily. Some users are wary of web forms, however, assuming that submitting their email addresses through one will expose them to spam. You should therefore also include a visible email address they can alternatively use (which would be protected from spammers, of course—we'll explain how to do that later). The visibility of your email address also adds to your credibility, which is less of an issue if your site is a blog, but is essential if you are selling from your website.

You should also include a telephone number on your contact page, if you want people to be able to reach you this way. Bricks-and-mortar businesses should also include a real, physical street address (not a P.O. box) to reinforce their status as an established, credible, real-world entity.

OTHER PAGES YOU MAY NEED ON YOUR SITE

> "Portfolio" (for creatives, to showcase your works)
> "Delivery Information" and "Returns Policy" (if your products require physical shipping), and "Terms & Conditions" (if you're selling online)
> "Privacy Policy," "Cookies," etc. (see the "Legal Issues" section in Chapter 10)

Maple Leaf Music's "Contact" page shows their telephone number, address, and email address clearly (as well as providing a web form), and a link to a map and directions are also provided. (http://www.mapleleafmusic.com)

Writing for the web

Writing for the web is different from writing for print. When crafting your text, bear the following in mind.

> People's attention spans are shorter these days, and even more so when reading onscreen—so don't make it too wordy. Use headings and short, digestible paragraphs.
> Important points should be visible straight away.
> With the above in mind, the journalistic "inverted pyramid" style works well when writing your pages. Begin with the conclusion first, then the supporting information.
> People are impatient, so give them what they are looking for—your contact details, maybe also your prices—without making them jump through hoops to find it. Otherwise, they may click away.
> Think of benefits, not features. Turn your copy round to make it customer-centric: instead of describing the details of your service, describe how it will help your customer.
> Include "calls to action"—make use of phrases such as: "click here," "contact me," "sign up for my newsletter," etc.
> Make sure your blog-post headings are enticing. Otherwise people won't click on them, and your posts won't get read.
> You need to make sure your website text is keyword-rich so you'll be found in Google and the other search engines. (I'll explain more about this and SEO—search engine optimization—in Chapter 9.)

Finding and USING IMAGES

Whatever type of website you're building, you'll need to include images. Even for the most serious business website, you'll need some visual interest to engage your visitors.

If you look at some commercial websites, you'll see that very often an image is used to underline each of the company's or product's unique selling points, whether this is done using a rotating header panel with writing on each of the image slides, or simply pictures interspersed throughout the text.

YOU CAN USE:

> your own photos, either scanned, or taken with a digital camera or cell phone
> photos from a stock-photo library, which are very reasonable in cost

Images for the web should be in .jpg (.jpeg), .png, or .gif format.

Some ideas of types of images you can use for business websites are:

> conceptual photographs (for example, skies, puzzles, keys, a handshake, building blocks, a soaring plane, a parachute, smiling people—or your own, more original, ideas)
> decorative photographs (such as flowers, landscapes, or seascapes)
> pictures of the location or the town where you're based (this could be local landmarks, buildings, street scenes, etc.)

Beautiful illustrations from Shutterstock, Inc. / Shutterstock.com.

Some good places to get stock photos for use on your site are:
http://www.istockphoto.com
http://www.fotolia.com
http://www.shutterstock.com
http://www.clipart.com*

*This one works out as very inexpensive if you figure out what you need in advance—you're allowed up to 250 images in a week at a flat rate of $14.95, as at time of writing.)

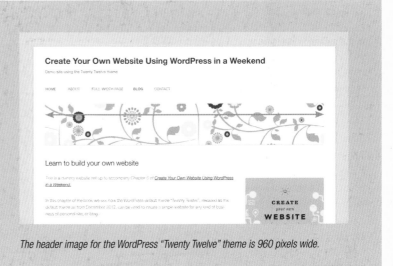

The header image for the WordPress "Twenty Twelve" theme is 960 pixels wide.

Consider using illustrations rather than photographs (also available from stock-image sources)—they can look more individual.

Get some ideas from other sites in your domain (whether you like or dislike their choices), and also look at the images used in WordPress themes (see page 90), as these always incorporate dummy visuals.

WORKING ON YOUR OWN PHOTOS
You don't need to buy special image-editing software to create your site. WordPress includes a built-in resizing, rotating, and cropping mechanism, and with the default theme we'll use for the model website, you can crop your photos for the header area through an easy-to-use interface.

However, you may need to work on your images in order to create a custom header image—perhaps one that incorporates your logo or your business name. For this, I suggest

you either use an online photo-editor such as Pixlr (http://pixlr.com) or download Gimp, a free software for both Mac and PC. We'll go through each step of creating a custom header with Pixlr in Chapter 5.

Digital photographs are huge in size. If your hosting package offers you limited storage space, it may be practical to reduce the size of your digital images before uploading them. Again, you can use Pixlr to do this. Open the photographs, reduce the image size (by half, for example—check the guidelines that follow to make sure you don't reduce them too much), and save them to your computer before uploading them to WordPress.

IMAGE SIZE
Images for websites are measured in pixels. To give you an idea, the header image of the WordPress "Twenty Twelve" theme is 960 pixels wide. So, when purchasing or preparing

an image for your website header image, 960 pixels is the maximum width you will need.

If you're purchasing stock photos for the pages of your website, rather than the header image, you will be able to buy small, or even extra-small, images. It is unlikely that your photos will ever need to be wider than 630 pixels, so choose a size that accommodates this easily.

You won't normally need to resize your photographs before you upload them to the site; WordPress does this for you. The above sizing guideline is to bear in mind when purchasing stock images or when reducing the size of images yourself, in order to save space on your site.

DO YOU NEED A LOGO FOR YOUR SITE?
Not every website needs an actual logo. One way to brand yourself without using a logo is to choose

TIP

If you're selling products from your website, consider getting professional photos taken—it can make a big difference as to how professional your site looks.

a distinctive font and then use it for your name or the site's title on your header panel—we'll show you how to do this in Chapter 5.

If you want to get a logo made, try:

> buildabrand.com—This is an online brand-builder that lets you create and download a logo on the spot. It's a free service, but if you want to use the logo for your business cards as well, or have it appear on a transparent background to overlay on a different-colored header, you'll need to pay $35.

> 99designs.com—You submit your "design brief," and then let dozens of designers from around the globe enter the competition to design your logo. You pick the one you like best, and if you don't like any of them, you simply get your money back. (The process takes a week, so this is something to think about beforehand.) They also have a "logo store" that you can browse and choose a design that they will then customize for you within 24 hours.

instant online logo maker at http://buildabrand.com

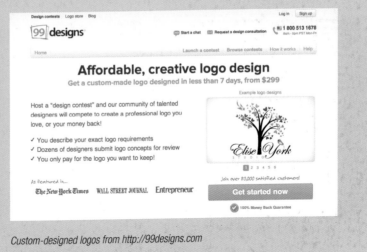

Custom-designed logos from http://99designs.com

IMAGE COPYRIGHT

Don't take photographs from other people's websites without their permission—you're not allowed to, there could be copyright issues, and you may find yourself slapped with a lawsuit. Stock photos are so inexpensive that it simply isn't worth it.

"Gypsy Garden" by Jen Furlotte, available from http://pixelsandicecream.deviantart.com

"Lil Tree," "Abstract," and "Paper" by http://backgrounds.mysitemyway.com. A Google search for "free website backgrounds" will bring up dozens of sites where you can get background designs like the ones above. (Remember to credit the designer, if this is required.)

BACKGROUND IMAGES

Most themes let you add images to the background of your site; this is a very good way of adding individuality. For a blog-style site, one of your own photographs might be suitable, but you may prefer a pattern, or something more sober for a business site.

PLACES TO FIND BACKGROUNDS
http://www.patterncooler.com
http://www.colourlovers.com
http://www.backgroundlabs.com
http://subtlepatterns.com

Video and AUDIO

Adding videos to your website is a very popular way of adding life to it. In order to show a video on your site, it has to be hosted by a third-party site such as YouTube or Vimeo; once hosted, WordPress makes it very easy to "embed" videos into your site so that they actually appear on your own web page, rather than the visitor having to go to another site to watch it.

Hosting your video on YouTube or Vimeo is also a great way of attracting new clientele.

Audio can also be included in a similar way, although the result isn't yet quite as smooth; we'll look at including both video and audio in Chapter 5.

THIRD-PARTY SITES
Content can easily be added to your site from the following third-party sites:
YouTube
Vimeo
DailyMotion
Flickr (both videos and images)
SoundCloud (via a plugin)

You can easily incorporate videos on your website by hosting them on YouTube.

4

Setting up WordPress

YOU'VE PLANNED OUT THE WEBSITE YOU'RE GOING TO BUILD; NOW IT'S TIME START CREATING IT. THE FIRST THING YOU NEED TO DO IS TO SET UP WORDPRESS.

The one-click INSTALL

These instructions refer to the setup of the self-hosted version of WordPress; if you're planning on using WordPress.com, please see over the page.

If you've followed the advice given previously and chosen one of the suggested hosting companies, or an alternative hosting company with a one-click install system, it will now be extremely easy to set up WordPress.

Here is how to install WordPress on Dreamhost. It will be a similar process with another host, although their one-click system may be slightly different.

1. **Log into Dreamhost.** Go to Goodies > One-Click Installs on the left-hand menu.
2. **Scroll down** the page a little and click on "WordPress."
3. **Click** the blue box labeled "Custom Installation."
4. **Select** your domain and click "Install it for me now!"
5. **Check your email** and look for an email from Dreamhost, which will arrive in just a few minutes. Click the first link in the email, underneath where it says, "Please create an admin user at:"
6. **On the web page**, fill in the details as follows:
   Site Title: Your business name or the name of your website (this can be changed later).

   Username: You can change this if you like, but it is fine to keep it as "admin."
   Password: As you like, but keep the details somewhere safe, as this will be the password you use each time you log in.
   Your email address: This will be the email address where you'll be informed of any updates to WordPress, so make sure it is your main email address.
   Privacy: Uncheck the box, as you don't want the search engines to visit your site until it is ready; we'll come back to this in Chapter 5. Now click "Install WordPress."
7. **You're done!** You can now log in.

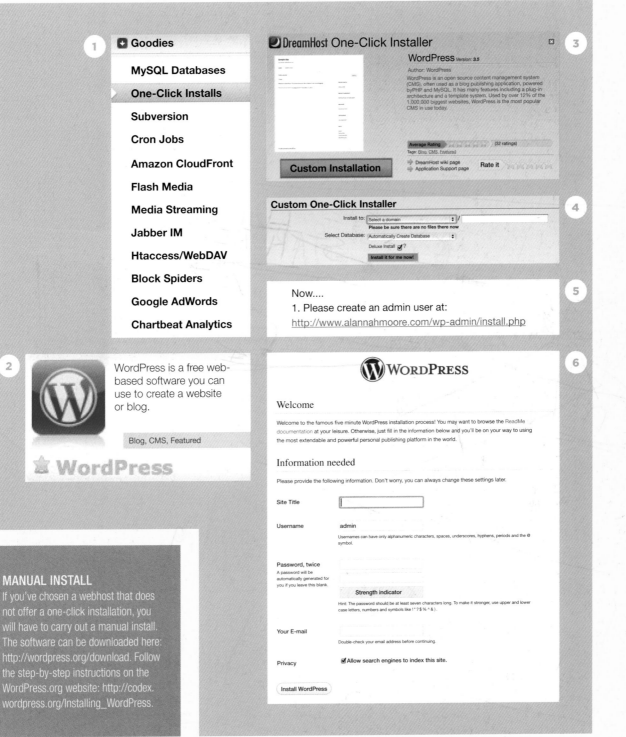

1

➕ Goodies

MySQL Databases

One-Click Installs

Subversion

Cron Jobs

Amazon CloudFront

Flash Media

Media Streaming

Jabber IM

Htaccess/WebDAV

Block Spiders

Google AdWords

Chartbeat Analytics

3

🌀 DreamHost One-Click Installer

WordPress *Version: 3.5*

Author: WordPress

WordPress is an open source content management system (CMS), often used as a blog publishing application, powered by PHP and MySQL. It has many features including a plug-in architecture and a template system. Used by over 12% of the 1,000,000 biggest websites, WordPress is the most popular CMS in use today.

Average Rating ★★★★★ (32 ratings)
Tags: Blog, CMS, Featured

Custom Installation

➡ DreamHost wiki page
➡ Application Support page   Rate it ★★★★★

4

Custom One-Click Installer

Install to: [Select a domain ▾] / [   ]
Please be sure there are no files there now

Select Database: [Automatically Create Database ▾]

Deluxe Install ☑ ?

[Install it for me now!]

5

Now....

1. Please create an admin user at:

http://www.alannahmoore.com/wp-admin/install.php

2

WordPress is a free web-based software you can use to create a website or blog.

Blog, CMS, Featured

⭐ **WordPress**

6

Ⓦ WORDPRESS

Welcome

Welcome to the famous five minute WordPress installation process! You may want to browse the ReadMe documentation at your leisure. Otherwise, just fill in the information below and you'll be on your way to using the most extendable and powerful personal publishing platform in the world.

Information needed

Please provide the following information. Don't worry, you can always change these settings later.

Site Title   [   ]

Username   admin

Usernames can have only alphanumeric characters, spaces, underscores, hyphens, periods and the @ symbol.

Password, twice
A password will be automatically generated for you if you leave this blank.

[   ]

[Strength indicator]

Hint: The password should be at least seven characters long. To make it stronger, use upper and lower case letters, numbers and symbols like ! " ? $ % ^ &).

Your E-mail   [   ]

Double-check your email address before continuing.

Privacy   ☑ Allow search engines to index this site.

[Install WordPress]

MANUAL INSTALL

If you've chosen a webhost that does not offer a one-click installation, you will have to carry out a manual install. The software can be downloaded here: http://wordpress.org/download. Follow the step-by-step instructions on the WordPress.org website: http://codex.wordpress.org/Installing_WordPress.

Setting up using WORDPRESS.COM

If you're going to use the hosted version of WordPress (WordPress.com), your setup will be even easier, and you'll have your blog up and running in just a few minutes.

1. Go to http://wordpress.com, click "Get Started," and sign up. Note when choosing your blog name, you will be able to upgrade to your own domain once you've signed up.

It's up to you whether you want to choose the "Value Bundle" at this stage (an upgrade including a domain name, extra space, a "No Ads" option, custom design, and an HD video option); if you're not certain just yet, you can always do it later, saving the same money if you buy the whole bundle. Click either "Upgrade" or "Create Blog" accordingly.

2. Once you've signed up, check your email inbox and click the blue "Activate Blog" button in the email you receive.

3. WordPress will now ask you to follow a series of steps to help you get up and running with your blog, but if you're not ready to complete any of the steps right now, that isn't a problem—just click "Next Step;" you can come back to any of these later on. You'll be asked:

i. Which topics you'd like to follow (other people's blogs that you might be interested in reading)

ii. Whether to let the system find your friends' WordPress blogs (and at the same time choose whether you want to publish

The WordPress.com administration gives you plenty of tips when you first log in to help you get started—a video, a "Zero to hero" guide, and links to support documentation (3).

your blog posts automatically on Facebook or Twitter)

iii. To set up your blog title and tagline; and choose your language

iv. To choose and customize a theme

v. To create your first post.

When you've finished, or when you've simply clicked through the steps, you'll

find yourself at your WordPress "home page." From this area, you can read other blog posts and check your blog stats; there is also a quick link to post to your blog ("New Post," top right), which you may find useful later, but for now, to finish customizing and setting up your blog, you'll need to log into your administration area. Do this by clicking "My Blogs" at the top of the screen, and then "Blog Admin" underneath the title of your blog.

You are now inside your admin area (see screenshot No. 3 opposite). Clicking the links at the top left of the screen will let you toggle back and forth between your live site and the admin area (1). The navigation on the left-hand side will take you to the different areas of the administration (2). Clicking your user name at the top right (4) will take you back to your WordPress home page.

FIRST STEPS

1. **Domain**—if your site is to carry any weight, you must have your own domain name. You may want to familiarize yourself a little further with the system before you commit; when you are ready, go to Store > Domains, and follow the instructions. (Your domain can also be purchased as part of the "Value Bundle.")

2. **Settings**—Alter the title and tagline of your site and set the time zone on the Settings > General page.

3. **Profile**—Fill in details about yourself at Users > My Profile.

4. **Theme**—If you skipped this step during the setup, you can now choose your theme by going to Appearance > Themes. You'll find the customization options in the Appearance > Theme Options, Header and Background areas (options vary theme to theme).

See the example site at http://create yourwebsiteinaweekend.wordpress.com

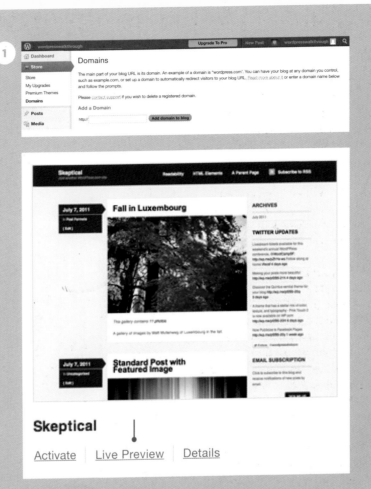

To help you choose your theme, WordPress offers you a "Live Preview" option that lets you play around with the colors and the header, and with certain other elements (depending on the theme), before you choose to go live with it.

Starting to blog

1. **Create** your first post at Posts > Add New. (You'll also want to delete the existing dummy post from the Posts > All Posts page.)

2. **Create** any pages you want to add to the site (for example, an "About" page) in the Pages > New Page area.

3. **Add sidebar** widgets (including Facebook and Twitter, if you use them) by going to Appearance > Widgets.

4. **Categorize** your posts at Posts > Categories.

5. **Customize** your menu at Appearance > Menus.

6. **Check** and reply to your comments in the "Comments" area.

5

Step-by-step: creating a basic model website

YOU'VE PLANNED YOUR SITE AND YOU'VE SET UP WORDPRESS. WE'RE NOW GOING TO SEE HOW TO CREATE A BASIC WEBSITE.

This walkthrough uses the WordPress default theme. We can consider this a "starter recipe" from which you can move on to more advanced setups once you have mastered the basics. The current default theme has a clean, simple, and attractive design, and you may find this is the perfect theme for your website. Some of you may want to start immediately on something more complex; do follow the walkthrough in its entirety, however, as you will learn things here that you will need to know later on, when customizing a more complex template.

Introducing the default WORDPRESS THEME "TWENTY TWELVE"

1. **The title and tagline or header text.** Here is where you put your business name and an optional short subtitle. You can change the font color, or choose an image header instead and omit the text.
2. **The background.** You can change its color or upload an image to use.
3. **The menu.** You can create levels of drop-down menus. These only appear when the user runs their mouse over the main menu item.
4. **The page text.** Here you can have introductory text or blog posts.
5. **Footer widgets.** This isn't standard in every theme, but this theme gives you the option to include widgets (small elements of content; see no. 9) at the bottom of the home page.
6. **The footer.** This theme links to the WordPress website, but you could put your name and copyright notice in this space as well.
7. **The header panel or image.** It's optional to include an image, known as a header, at the top, as well as, or instead of, the header text. If you choose a header image,

it will appear on all pages of the site. This one is purely decorative, but you may want to include a logo or business name in yours.

8. **The sidebar.** Your blog pages include a column to the right-hand side, but for the main pages, you you may choose to omit the sidebar and have the text cover the full width of the site.

9. **Sidebar widgets.** You can put any content you like in the sidebar. It's great for things like testimonials, special offers, social media buttons (see page 143), or your latest blog or news posts.

You can see the demo site live online here: http://www.createyourwebsiteinaweekend.com/twentytwelve

The "Twenty Twelve" default theme
> Has a clean and modern, uncluttered feel
> Can be made your own with a number of customization options
> Is "responsive", so it looks great on a smartphone or a tablet
> Is suitable for many kinds of website—personal, business or blog.

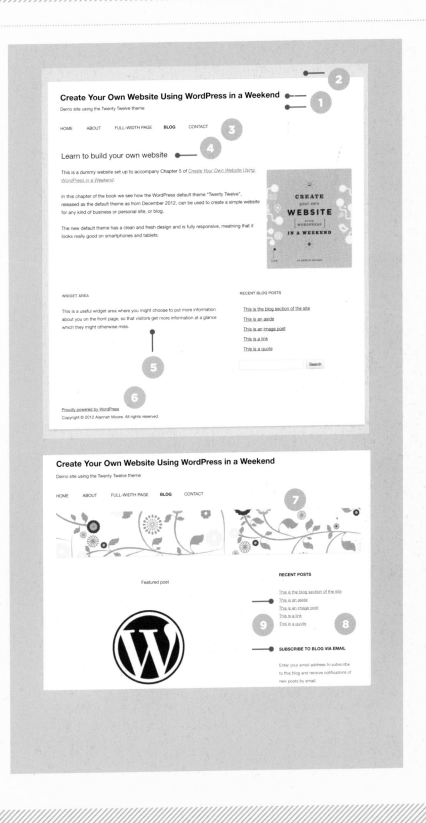

The live site and ADMIN AREA

The first thing to understand when working with WordPress is that there are two distinct areas of your website. The first is the live website, which is visible by going to your domain. The second is the admin area, which cannot be seen or accessed by visitors to your website, only by you or others you choose to add as administrators.

Your admin area—also referred to as the back end—can be accessed here: http://www.yourdomain.com/wp-login.php.

When you are customizing a WordPress website, you make changes to your website in the admin area, and you can then see those changes on the live website. You will need to switch back and forth between the two areas while you are customizing your site.

Once you are logged in to WordPress, the front page of your site will show a dark gray strip at the top of it (other people won't see this when they visit your site) that allows you to switch back and forth between the live site and the admin area, so you can make changes and then check how they look.

The strip offers you various choices that will become familiar once you are more accustomed to working with WordPress. If you click on

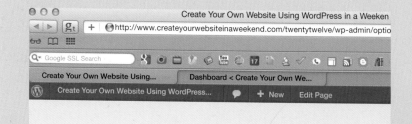

The Dashboard can be accessed from the dark gray strip that appears on your site once you're logged in.

You may find it easy to work with two tabs open, one showing the live website, and the other showing the admin area. Refresh the page on the live website to see how your changes look.

"Dashboard," it will take you to your admin area's home page.

An alternative way to work with WordPress is to have the site open in one tab, and the admin area open in another tab. I find this the easiest way to make changes and check how they look, but it is up to you how you choose to work.

The ADMIN AREA

This is how your dashboard—or the home page of your admin area—will look when you first log into it.

On your left, you will see a navigation column (1) that takes you to different admin areas. If you click on one of the items, you will see that a series of sub-menu items becomes visible. These options are also visible if you roll your mouse over them.

The larger, main area of the page (2) is where you will actually do your editing or your customization, according to which part of the admin area you are working in.

The Dashboard is the home page of your admin area.

This is the screen you will use when you are adding a new page to your site. The left-hand navigation is visible wherever you are inside the admin area, so you can easily find your way around.

TIP

You will want to bookmark the web address of your admin area so you can come back to it easily. Bookmark this page: http://www.yourdomain.com/wp-admin (obviously substitute your real domain name!). If you check the box labeled "Remember Me" when logging in, you can go straight into the admin area each time you visit, without having to log in.

First STEPS

At this point you're probably keen to dive into the fun part of customizing your new demo site, but before you begin, you need to carry out a few preliminary steps.

You've probably noticed that there are several useful links on the dashboard inviting you to begin setting up your website. You will be able to explore these at your leisure, but for the purposes of this walkthrough, we will follow a series of steps that will help you to get up and running more quickly.

Remember that WordPress is a very full-featured software that can be made to do all kinds of things. As you navigate around the admin area, you will see many different options offered to you. For now, you only need to follow the steps in the walkthrough. Other, more complex setups will require you to implement some of these alternative options, but for our initial purposes, you won't need them.

STEP 1: GENERAL SETTINGS

1. **On the left-hand** navigation, click Settings > General.
2. **Here you can change** the site title and tagline that you set up during the installation, as well as the email address where the WordPress update notifications will get sent.

3. **You can also change** the time zone to correspond to where you are, so that your blog or news posts are stamped with the correct time.
4. **You don't need to change** anything else on this page. When you have finished, click the blue "Save Changes" button.

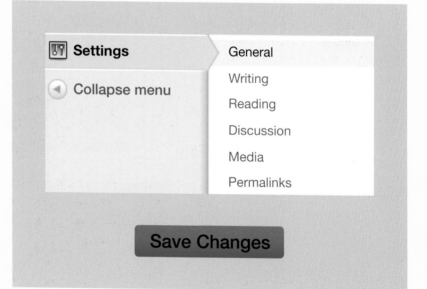

STEP 2: SEARCH ENGINES

You're setting up a dummy site, so you don't want the search engines to visit your website just yet. When you're done setting up your real, live site, you will certainly want it listed, but until then it's best to keep your site under wraps.

1. **In the navigation,** go to Settings > Reading.
2. **Check** the checkbox next to "Discourage search engines from indexing this site."
3. **Click** the blue "Save Changes" button.

STEP 3: COMMENTS

1. Click Settings > Discussion.

Here, you can decide on your own default setting—whether or not you want to allow people to leave comments on your site. The setting can be overridden for individual pages, so your decision isn't definitive; it's more a matter of what is convenient for you.

It's my guess that you won't want people to leave comments on the main pages of your site, but for your blog (news) posts, you will. If this is the case, you can disable the comments for now. When your site is set up and you have finished creating the main pages of your site, you can come back here and enable the comments. That way, when you add your blog or news posts, the comments will be enabled automatically for your blog section.

2. So, to disable comments, uncheck the box next to "Allow people to post comments on new articles."

(You may have a question at this point concerning spam messages or unwanted comments displaying on your site. There is a simple way to prevent this happening, which we will address a little later when we're looking at plugins.)

3. At this stage, you don't have to change anything else on this page, so you can click the blue "Save Changes" button.

Discussion Settings

Default article settings

☐ Attempt to notify any blobs linked to from the article

☑ Allow link notifications from other blogs (pingbacks and trackbacks)

☐ Allow people to post comments on new articles

(These settings may be overridden for individual articles.)

TRACKBACKS AND PINGBACKS

Trackbacks and pingbacks are notifications you receive when another blog has linked to your site content. Unfortunately, these notifications are very often spam, so you may want to uncheck the checkbox next to "Allow link notifications" so that you don't receive them.

STEP 4: YOUR NAME ON YOUR BLOG OR NEWS POSTS

1. Go to Users > Your Profile. When you post a news item in your blog area, it will show up as having been posted by "admin," unless you choose to set it to something that looks more personal.

2. Add your first name and surname into the appropriate fields, and look at the drop-down menu below—you will see that various arrangements of your name have magically appeared as options to choose from. You may not want your real name to show on the site, however—in which case, type a nickname into the nickname field and select it on the drop-down.

3. There is no need to change anything else now, so just click the blue "Save Changes" button at the bottom when you've finished.

Name

Username	admin	*Usernames cannot be changed.*
First Name		
Last Name		
Nickname *(required)*	admin	
Display name publicly as	admin	

How to get a gravatar

In order to have your own picture show up when you respond to a blog comment, you need to get a "gravatar." This means a "globally recognized avatar"—in other words, an image of your own choosing, tied to your email address, that will show up wherever you post on the web using the same email address. To set up yours, go to http://en.gravatar.com (for different languages click the "Languages" link down at the bottom of the page).

When you have the Jetpack plugin installed on your site (see page 75), site visitors will be able to find out more about the profile of commenters who also have gravatars by hovering over their image. You can enable this in Settings > Discussion. You can also put a gravatar image of yourself in the sidebar.

One thought on "This is an image post"

Alannah
October 31, 2012 at 5:57 pm

What a beautiful picture of Venice. I was there last October.

One thought on "This is an image post"

STEP 5: PERMALINKS

The last thing to do in the "First Steps" section is to change your permalinks—that is, the web addresses of new pages you are going to create in WordPress. If you change nothing here, you will find your new web pages are allocated strange-looking web addresses like http://www.yourdomain.com/?page_id=2. These don't look very tidy, but more importantly, they mean nothing to search engines, and therefore will not help drive traffic to your site.

If you make the following change, your web addresses will look something like this instead: http://www.yourdomain.com/contact/.

1. **Go to** Settings > Permalinks.
2. **Check** the radio button next to "Post name."
3. **As before**, click the blue button at the bottom when you're done.

You are now ready to move onto the fun part of the customization—changing the way your website looks.

Permalink Settings

By default WordPress uses web URLs which have question marks and lots of numbers min them, however WordPress offers you the ability to create a custom URL stucture aesthetics, usability, and forward-compatibility of your links. A number of tags are available, and here are some examples to get you started.

Common Settings

○ Default	http://www.createyourwebsiteinaweekend.com/twentytwelve/?p=123
○ Day and name	http://www.createyourwebsiteinaweekend.com/twentytwelve/2013/01/13/sample-post/
○ Month and name	http://www.createyourwebsiteinaweekend.com/twentytwelve/2013/01/sample-post/
○ Numeric	http://www.createyourwebsiteinaweekend.com/twentytwelve/archives/123
● Post name	http://www.createyourwebsiteinaweekend.com/twentytwelve/sample-post/
○ Custom Structure	http://www.createyourwebsiteinaweekend.com/twentytwelve

The HEADER

Appearance
Plugins
Users
Tools
Settings
Collapse menu

Themes
Widgets
Menus
Header
Background
Editor

Click on Appearance > Header on the left-hand navigation.

You will be taken to a page like the one below.

Create Your Own Website Using WordPress...   + New   Howdy, admin

Dashboard
Posts
Media
Pages
Comments
Appearance
Themes
Widgets
Menus
Header
Background
Editor
Plugins
Users
Tools
Settings
Collapse menu

Custom Header   Help ▾

Header Image

Preview

Create Your Own Website Using WordPress in a Weekend

Demo site using the Twenty Twelve theme

Select Image

You can select an image to be shown at the top of your site by uploading from your computer or choosing from your media library. After selecting an image you will be able to crop it.

Suggested width is 960 pixels. Suggested height is 250 pixels.

Choose an image from your computer:

Choose File   no file selected   Upload

Or choose an image from your media library.

Choose Image

Header Text

Header Text   ☑ Show header text with your image.

Text Color   [ ] Select Color

Save Changes

This page is where you choose whether your site will have:
> a text heading
> a text heading with a header image beneath it

> just a header image, which incorporates your website title or business name, and your logo, if you are going to use one

Have a look at the example screenshots to see how the different layouts appear, then play around with the options to decide which is best for your own site.

OPTION 1: A TEXT HEADING

The clean design of the default theme ensures that your website title, or business name, looks attractive simply written in text at the top of the page, as you can see in the screenshot right.

If you choose the text-only option, you will want to add some visual interest on the front page by adding a picture alongside your home page text, as I have done here.

To choose the text-only option that you can see here, you don't need to do anything as this is the default setting. (On the "Custom Header" page, the checkbox next to "Show header text with your image" should already be ticked.)

Remember that if you want to change the header text or subtitle, the place to do it is in Settings > General.

To change the color of the text:

1. **In the "Header Text"** area of the page, click on the box labeled "Select Color," and a color-picker device will appear.
2. **Click once** inside the square, and move the slider up or down the color column to the right until you're in the range of colors you're looking for. Fine-tune your choice within the square. You can preview the color you're choosing at the top of the page. (Click the "Default" button if you need to go back to where you started.)
3. **When you've chosen** your heading color, click "Save Changes."

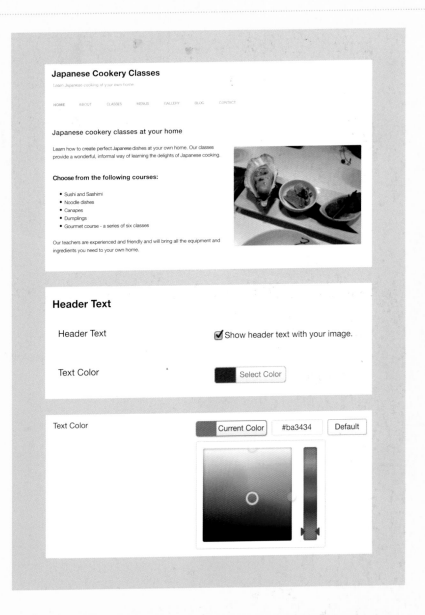

WEBSITE COLORS

Web colors are defined using a "hexadecimal code" of six letters and numbers (sometimes shortened to three). This is the code you can see next to the hash sign (#) in the image above. The code #FFFFFF means white, and #000000 means black. There is no need to remember these, but using "hex" codes can be a useful way of making elements match exactly, if you want them to.

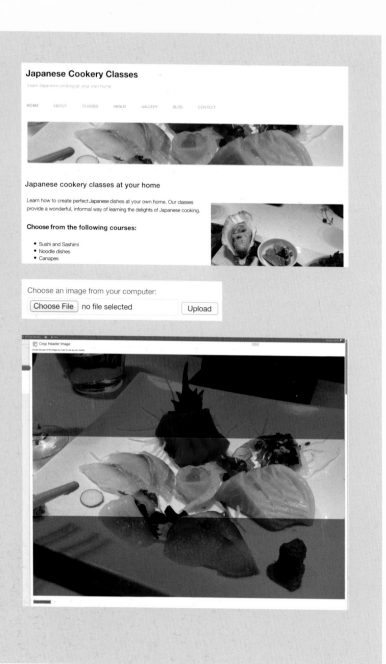

OPTION 2: A TEXT HEADING WITH A HEADER IMAGE

Adding an image to the header area is a really good way of making your site look unique.

However attractive a header image can look, including one won't be the best choice for all websites, particularly business ones. I decided for my live demo website not to have a header image, but to make the page visually interesting by including an image of the book cover next to the home page text instead (see page 39, or the live site at http://www.createyourwebsiteinaweekend.com/twentytwelve).

You can add any image you like to the header area, and you can even upload several images, which will mean your site visitors will see different, random, images shown in the header area as they surf around the pages of your site. This is an interesting and fun touch, particularly suitable for a personal website or a blog.

To add a header image:

1. **Underneath** "Choose an image from your computer," click the "Choose File" button.

Navigate to the image you want to use on your computer, select it, and click "Choose" or "Open," depending on whether you are using a Mac or a PC. Then click the "Upload" button.

2. Now, choose the area of the image you want to use for the header—see opposite.

You can move the selected area around and resize it by moving the borders with your mouse. (If you lose your selected area, just click and select again; if you are uploading a digital photo, you will need to scroll to the right to include the full width of the image.)

When you're happy with what you've selected, click "Crop and Publish." (Do not worry if the area you have selected looks huge—the system will automatically resize it to fit the width of the site.)

3. When you see the yellow "Header updated" notice at the top of the screen, go to your live site to see your new header in position.

To display random images:
If you choose the random option, your site visitors will see a different header image displayed on each page they visit.

1. Upload and crop some more header images in the usual way.
2. Click the radio button next to "Random: Show a different image on each page."
3. Click the "Save Changes" button at the bottom of the page.

⦿ **Random:** Show a different image on each page.

Deleting header images
If you upload a header image and find it doesn't look good, you can easily delete it by going to Media > Library. Hover your mouse over the thumbnail of the image you want to remove, and click on the red "Delete Permanently" link that appears. (You will need to delete headers you don't want to show if you are choosing the random option, as the system will show all headers that are uploaded.)

cropped-IMG_2554.jpg - Header Image
JPG

Edit | Delete Permanently | View

RESIZING YOUR HEADER IMAGES
If you're going with the random images option, you may want to make sure all your header images are the same size, so that when your site visitor browses from page to page, the transition is smooth. Unfortunately, cropping images as you upload them inside the "Custom Header" area doesn't allow you to see the dimensions of the crop area, which makes it impossible to match sizes at the upload stage. To make them all the same size, you can either change their size once they've been uploaded to the Media Library (see page 66), before selecting them as header images, or you can do it before you upload the images, using an image-editing tool such as Pixlr to crop them at the same size (see the next page for info on how to use Pixlr). Image headers need to be 960 pixels in width, and can be any height you choose.

OPTION 3: JUST A HEADER IMAGE

If you choose to leave out the text heading and put only an image at the top of your website pages, you will want to incorporate your website title and/or logo into it so that your site has a heading. This, you can't do inside WordPress—you'll need to use an external image-editor such as Pixlr (see below).

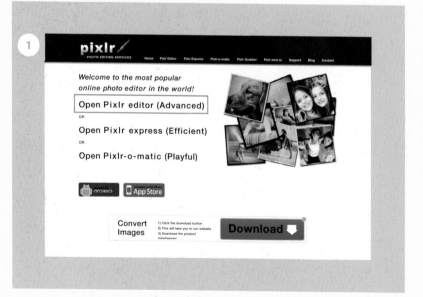

To add a header image:

1. **Upload your header**, as per Option 2 before.
2. **Uncheck** the text box next to "Show header text with your image."
3. **Click the blue** "Save Changes" button and check how your website looks.

How to create a header using Pixlr.

1. **Go to** http://pixlr.com and click on "Open Pixlr editor (Advanced)."
2. **Choose** "Open image from computer."

Navigate to the image on your computer and select it, so that it opens up in Pixlr.

3. **If you** are using a digital photo for your background, before you do anything you will need to reduce the size of your image. Go to Image > Image size.

4. If you want to use the entire width of your photograph for your header, set the width at 960 pixels. If you only want to use part of it, try it slightly larger at, for example, 1200 pixels (you may need to experiment a little to get the right size). Keep the box next to "Constrain proportions" checked, so that the image doesn't become distorted; do not change the figure given for the height, as this will adjust automatically.

5. Select the crop tool from the toolbar you can see on the left.

In the "Crop options" area, choose "Aspect ratio" from the "Constraint" drop-down, and select your width and height options. The width needs to be set at 960 if it is to go right across the top of the website; you can set the height at whatever you choose. The suggested header height for the default theme is 250, however I feel that for a business site, a narrower header often looks better. Here, I am choosing to create a narrow header of just 125 pixels.

6. With your mouse, select the area you wish to use for the header. Once you have made a selection, you can reposition it by dragging it. Here, I'm using the entire width of the image, but you may not wish to; the proportions will remain correct if you choose a smaller area.

7. Click anywhere outside the image, then click the "Yes" button when asked to confirm the change.

8. Before you go any further, make sure you're seeing the header at its actual size. Type "100" in the percentage area at the bottom left of the image window, and press "Enter."

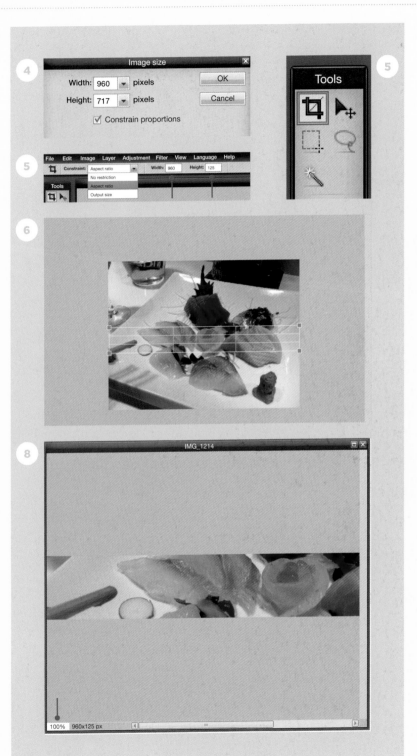

Then make the window larger by grabbing and enlarging from the bottom right corner, so that you can see the full width of the header.

9. Next, you'll need to add some lettering. Select the type tool from the left-hand toolbar.

10. Click inside the image, and a window will appear.

Type your header text into the text box. The options below let you choose the font, the size, and whether the text is in bold or italic. Click the "Color" box to choose the color of the text.

There are a number of ways you can choose the color, of which the "HSL" and "IMG" tabs will probably be the most useful. "HSL" stands for "Hue, Saturation, Lightness," and is just another of several ways used to describe color. In this tab you can choose colors from a color wheel similar to the one we've seen in WordPress. The "IMG" tab gives you a selection of colors picked out from the image. You can also move your mouse over the image and select a color directly from it, or type a six-number color code into the box if you want it to match another color you're going to use on your website See box on "Website Colors," page 47.

11. When you are happy with the look of the header, click File > Save (from the Pixl menu—not your internet browser menu!).

Name the file and save it to your computer, choosing jpeg format and 100% quality.

The HSL tab of the color picker.

The IMG tab of the color picker.

12. Finally, upload the file to your website, not forgetting to unselect the header text option, as you won't want it to appear there as well as the header.

Incorporating a logo into your header

Note that you will need your logo on a transparent background before you begin, if you are going to put it on a background other than white.

1. **Open** the Pixlr editor as before and choose "Create a new image."
2. **Name** the new file "header," and type the width and height in the boxes. As before, your width will need to be 960 pixels; for the height, make your choice (here, I have set a height of 125 pixels). (Ignore the drop-down titled "Presets".) When you are finished, click "OK."
3. **Click** the large rectangle at the bottom of the left-hand toolbar.

Select the background color of your header from the color picker that comes up, or type a "hex" color code into the box if you have a color reference you want to match. Click "OK."

4. **Click** the paint bucket tool from the left-hand toolbar.
5. **Click** inside your header, and the color will change from white to the color you have chosen.
6. **Open** your logo file by choosing File > Open image (again from the Pixlr menu, not your internet browser menu) and selecting your logo from your computer. When it opens in Pixlr, you will notice your logo has a gray and white checked background; this is merely to indicate that the background is in fact transparent.
7. **Click** the marquee tool in the toolbar, which lets you select a rectangular area of an image.

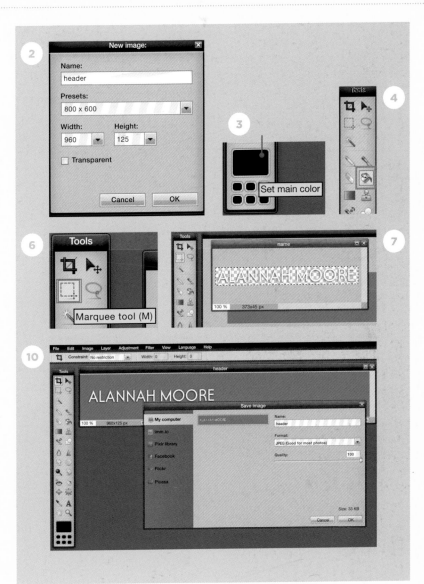

8. **Select** your logo by dragging your mouse across it.
9. **Click** Ctrl+C (PC) or Cmd+C (Mac) to copy the logo, then click inside the new header image, and click Ctrl+V (PC) or Cmd+V (Mac) to paste it in place.
10. **Use** your mouse to position the logo where you want it, then click File > Save (from the Pixlr menu), as before, saving the header to your computer at 100% quality.
11. **Upload** it to your website via the "Custom Header" area, not forgetting to uncheck the box next to "Show header text with your image."

The BACKGROUND

You've customized the header part of your website; now it's time to look at the background.

Click on Appearance > Background.

From this page, you can either upload an image file that will act as a page background, or choose a different background color.

For a more personal site or a blog, a background image or pattern can work really well, as it will make your site look completely unique. For a business site, I recommend a plain color—a background can work, but make sure the one you choose is subtle.

Appearance

Themes

Widgets

Menus

Edit CSS

Header

Background

Editor

To upload an image for the background:

1. Click "Choose File," and then select the image you want to use from your computer. When you have made your choice, click "Upload."

2. Having uploaded an image, you now have a few options:

If you have chosen an image taken with a digital camera as your background, the image is likely to be large enough to cover the entire computer screen, so none of the position or tile (repeat) settings will apply.

If your image is smaller than the screen area, you can choose whether to repeat it horizontally or vertically, "tile" the screen entirely with it, or position it to the left, right, or center of the screen. If you're unsure, experiment with the different settings to see how these look,

Display Options

Position	◉ Left ○ Center ○ Right
Repeat	○ No Repeat ◉ Tile ○ Tile Horizontally ○ Tile Vertically
Attachment	○ Scroll ◉ Fixed

but it's most likely that you'll want it to tile.

Clicking the radio button next to "Scroll" will make the background move as well as the page when the visitor scrolls down it. I recommend the "Fixed" option, as this keeps the background in the same position while you scroll down the pages, but you can try out both and see which one you prefer.

3. Click the "Save Changes" button when you've made your choice.

To change the background color:

1. As before, when you changed the color of your header text, click on "Select a Color" and choose the color you want using the color picker.

2. Click the "Save Changes" button when you're done.

Creating PAGES

Now that you have the basic appearance of your site in place, you are ready to move onto the content. Let's see how to create pages for your site.

You've probably noticed that WordPress has created a sample page for you; we need to delete this before we begin. **Click on Pages > All Pages, which will take you to a page like the one on the right.**

At the moment, there is only one page listed because there is now only one page present—when you create more pages, they will all be listed here. Move your mouse over the title "Sample Page," and you will see some links appear—click on "Trash" and the page will be deleted. Now you can create the pages you want on your site. (We will look at how to rearrange the menu shortly, so don't worry, for now, if you see your pages appearing on your site in the wrong order on the menu.)

Let's start with your home page.

1. **Click** either the "Add New" button at the top of the page, or the "Add New" link in the left-hand navigation. **You will be taken to a page like the one on the right.**
2. **Type** "Home" in the title area (indicated).
3. **Look** in the "Page Attributes" box to the right of the screen. From the drop-down entitled "Template," select "Front Page Template." (Ignore everything else in this box.)
4. **Click** the blue "Publish" button. Repeat for the other pages you are planning to create, but omit

Step 3—for the other pages of your site, you don't need to apply the special front page template, as they'll automatically be saved with the regular, default layout.

You'll be able to fill in the content of your website pages in a minute—there's one step to carry out first—so create the pages and save them without any content for now.

Choosing your HOME PAGE

The default setup for WordPress is to display your blog posts on the front page. But it's very likely that if you are creating a site to showcase your business, this setup will not suit you—you will probably prefer to write some introductory text about your business on the home page instead (as discussed in Chapter 3), and keep the blog posts (if you are going to create a blog) in a separate area. If you want to create your own text for the front page and put the blog posts elsewhere, work though the following steps; if you want your blog posts on the front page, you can skip this section.

Reading Settings

Front page displays

○ Your latest posts

● A static page (select below)

Front page: Home

Posts page: Blog

1. **First**, make sure that you have created and saved a page entitled "Home" as explained on the previous page (it doesn't matter that at this stage it is still blank—you will be able to fill in your page content in just a moment).

2. **If you want** a blog section on your site, make sure you have also created and saved a blank page entitled "Blog," "News," or whatever title you may prefer. (This page should stay blank as it will simply contain your blog posts—you'll see what I mean in just a moment.)

3. **Go to** Appearance > Reading. Check the radio button next to "A static page;" select "Home" in the first drop-down which is labeled "Front page;" and the title of your blog page in the second, labeled "Posts page." (If you are not going

to create a blog section, just leave the second drop-down as it is.)

4. **Click** "Save Changes" at the bottom of the page. If you go to your live site, you'll see your new home page (which is currently empty) on the front page, and if you have created a blog section, you'll see that the dummy post that was previously on the front page is now there. When you've created your real blog posts, this is where they will appear.

Now we will look at the features of the text-editing area, so that you can put your content onto your site pages.

Working with the TEXT EDITOR

To add content to your pages, go to Pages > All Pages. Click the title of the page you want to edit (or the small "Edit" link that appears underneath it when you move your mouse over it), and you will be taken to the "Edit Page" area for that page.

Inside the "Edit Page" area, you'll see many formatting buttons that will be familiar to you from using Word or other text-editing software.

Over the page is a guide to the various items you can use when editing text.

(If you can't see both rows of buttons, click the button indicated above and the second row of buttons will appear beneath. This button is known as the "Kitchen Sink" button; the idea is not to clutter up too much of your screen with buttons that you may not need to use—but it can be confusing if you haven't come across it before.)

TEXT-EDITING OPTIONS

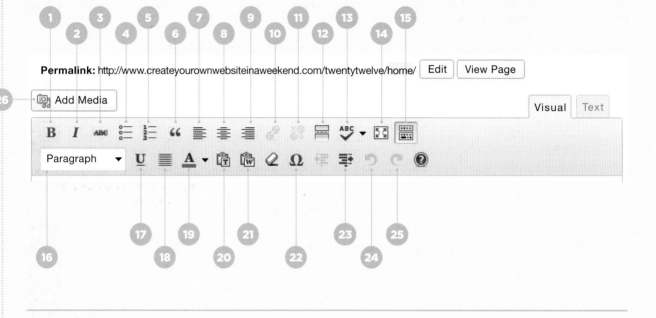

1, 2, 3, 17 Bold, italic, strikeout, and underline buttons.

4, 5 Bullet and numbered list keys.

6 Blockquote—a way of making your text stand out. Highlight the text you want to display in this way and then click the blockquote button.

7, 8, 9 Left-align, center, or right-align buttons.

18 Left or right justify button.

10, 11 Add or remove a link button. To add a link, select the text to be made into a link, click the link button, and a window will come up; then, type the web address in the "URL" field, check the box so the link will open in a new window, and click "Add Link" (see below right).

12 Inserts a "Read More" link (this does not work for pages; it is used only for blog posts).

13 Spell-checker button.

14 Full-screen button—it is sometimes easier to type with a full screen, as the text appears more clearly and there are fewer distractions.

15 The "Kitchen Sink" button.

16 Text style drop-down. Use this menu to format text. "Paragraph" will give you normal-sized text; the different heading options will give you various sizes for your headings, with "Heading 1" being the largest and most important on a page, and so on.

19 Text color button.

20, 21 These buttons are useful for copying and pasting text. If you want to copy text originally saved in a Word document, use the "W" button to paste it into the text area, otherwise it will bring extra code and formatting with it from the original. In the same way, use the "T" button to paste in text from software other than Word.

22 Insert special character button (this includes symbols such as the copyright symbol).

23 Indent paragraph button.

24, 25 Undo and re-do buttons (up to 10 actions).

26 Click this button to add media (i.e., images and audio)—we'll look at this on pages 62/67.

You will normally be working in the "Visual" view (see the tab in the image on the opposite page). Occasionally, you will need to access the coding of the page content, which you can do by clicking the "Text" tab.

When you have added text to each page, click the blue "Update" button. To view the page as it looks on the live site, click the "View Page" button (or access the pages via the menu on the website—don't worry that they aren't in the right order yet, as this is what we'll look at next). When you

are filling in the content for your pages, don't add anything to the blog page. This needs to be left completely blank; we'll see how to add blog posts a little later in this chapter.

TIP

Make use of the formatting options —this includes the heading hierarchy (16), as well as the lists (4), numbers (5), and blockquotes (6)—to make your text as clear as possible for site visitors to read. Remember what we said in Chapter 3 about the importance of clarity and accessibility of information on a website; how you format your text is a major part of this.

Adding pages to the MENU

With your pages in place, you now need to set up your menu so that the links to access these pages appear in a logical order. Until you set up the menu, your pages will appear in the menu in the order they were created.

1. **Go to** Appearance > Menus on the left-hand navigation.

2. **Create** a menu—type "Main" in the "Menu Name" field, and click the blue "Create Menu" button.

3. **To the left** of this area, look for a box entitled "Theme Locations." Select "Main" from the "Primary Menu" drop-down and click "Save."

4. **Scroll** down the page to where you can see a box entitled "Pages."

5. **Click** the "Select All" link and then the "Add to Menu" button. (If you can't see all your pages, click the "View All" link first.)

6. **You will see** all your pages added to the main area of the page; you can then drag them around to reorder them with your mouse. (Indenting a menu item will make it appear underneath the item above it as a drop-down.)

By convention, your "About" page usually goes after your home page link, and the "Contact" page last.

7. **When you're done,** click the blue "Save Menu" button. You can now go to your live website and see how your menu looks.

CREATING A MENU LABEL THAT'S DIFFERENT FROM A PAGE HEADING

You may want the heading visible on a page to be different from how it appears in the menu. For example, you won't want the heading "Home" to appear on your home page (whereas it should appear as "Home" in the menu). In the screenshot of the live demo site, we can see "Learn to build your own website" is the main heading, whereas the page is labeled "Home" in the menu.

To change the home page heading:

1. **Go to** the editing page for the home page (Pages > All Pages > Home).
2. **Change** the title of the page, and then click the "Update" button.
3. **Go back** to the "Menus" page (Appearance > Menus). You will see that the menu item has changed to the new title.
4. **Click** the small triangle you see to the right of the heading to open an options area, and in the "Navigation Label" field, type "Home" instead of the new home page heading.
5. **Click** the blue "Save Menu" button. Going back to your site's home page, you will see that the menu now says "Home," whereas the page is titled with its new heading.

ADDING NEW PAGES

When you add new pages from now on, they will not appear in the menu until you add them to it. To get them to appear automatically, check "Automatically add new top-level pages" (see image 3). Note you will still need to reorder the menu items each time you create pages.

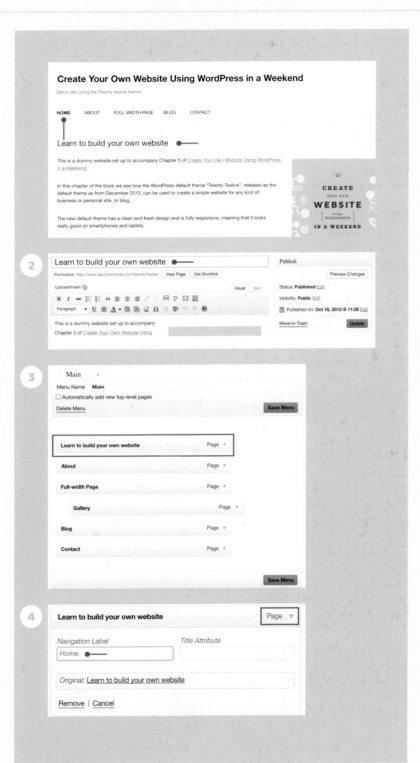

Adding images to YOUR SITE

We've seen how to create pages, work with the text editor, and how to add your pages to a menu. Now we will look at how you can add images to your pages.

ADDING IMAGES

To add an image to a page:

1. Click in the text-editing area where you want the image to appear.

2. Click the "Add Media" button above the editing buttons.

3. Click the "Select Files" button and navigate to the image you want to use on your computer. Select the image and click "Choose" or "Open," depending on whether you are using a Mac or a PC. (You can also add images by dragging them into the box where it says "Drop files anywhere to upload," if that is easier.)

4. Allow the image to upload. When it has uploaded, fill in the various fields as follows.

Type a title for the image in the "Title" and "Alt Text" fields. These will not be immediately visible on the page, however, if a viewer moves their mouse over the image, the title will show up. The "Alt Text" field will show up if the person visiting your site can't access images—this is not often the case, but you need to fill in the field as it provides information for Google. If you want a caption to be visible on the page, type it in the "Caption" field.

WordPress offers you the option of additionally displaying your image

on the site in a larger format, on its own page, if the visitor clicks on it (we'll see how to set this option in just a moment). If you want to do this, you can optionally type a description of the image that will show up only on the image's own page; type this in the field labeled "Description," otherwise you can leave it empty.

Set the alignment (that is, the positioning) of the image in the drop-down labeled "Alignment," underneath "Attachment Display Settings." In the example, I chose "Left," as I wanted the text to appear to the right of the image.

Scroll down inside the window; the next drop-down (screenshot opposite) is where you choose whether you

want to make the image link to something. Choosing "None" will obviously keep the image in its unlinked format; choose "Custom URL" if you want to link it to another web page, and paste in the web page address. "Attachment Page" is the setting you choose if you want to create a separate page displaying the image at larger size, plus any description. "Media File" will open the image at its original size in the browser window without any description.

Finally, you need to choose the size at which you want to display the image (you can fine tune this once the image is saved on the page).

5. When you've chosen your settings, click "Insert into page," then click the blue "Update"

button on your main editing page, and check how it looks on your live site.

6. If you want to make any changes or resize the image, click on the image in the text editing area. A button will appear at the top left; click on this to adjust the size, position, title, or caption. Take care not to click on the red button, as this will remove the image.)

7. Make your change and click "Update," remembering to also click the "Update" button on your editing page to save the change.

Note that you can use the size slider (indicated in the screenshot) to make the image smaller by incremental degrees of 10%. If you want to make it larger, you will need to upload it again at a larger size.

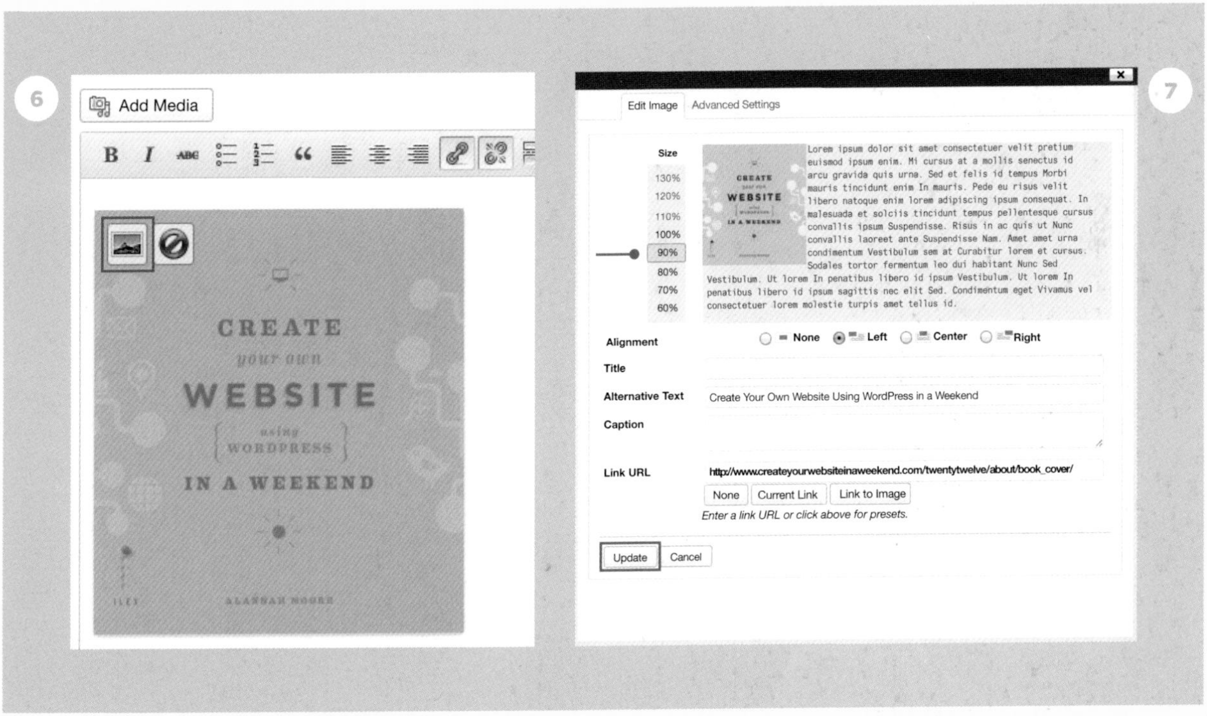

CREATING A GALLERY

WordPress has a neat feature that lets you create a gallery of images on your page.

1. Go to the page where you want to add the gallery, and then click inside the text box where you want the gallery to appear. Click the "Add Media" button.

2. When the window opens, click "Create Gallery" from the top left (as indicated).

Upload the images you wish to add to the gallery. You can add several simultaneously, either by selecting multiple images, or by dragging and dropping them into the box.

Should you experience any difficulty uploading several images at once, try uploading them in small batches. Click "Upload files" at the top of the window, wait for the batch to upload, then repeat for the next one.

(You can alternatively add images you've already uploaded by clicking the "Media Library" link at the top of the window. Select the images you want to include; use Ctrl + Click (PC)/Cmd + Click (Mac) to select multiple images.)

3. Click "Create a new gallery."

At this next screen, you can set your title and alt text for each image, and optionally also your caption and description (the description will show with the larger version of each image when clicked on from the gallery). You can reorder the images by dragging and dropping them. Alternatively, there is the option

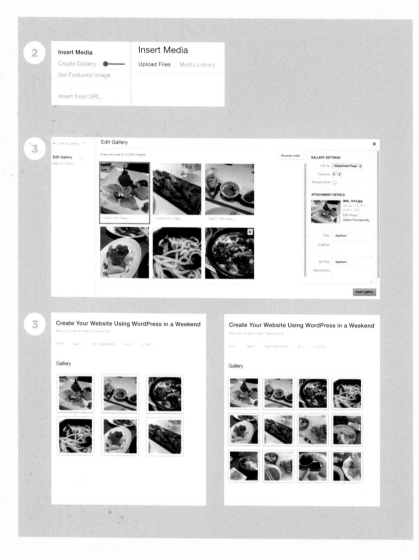

to have the thumbnails appear in random order—see the checkbox to the right under "Gallery Settings."

In the "Gallery Settings" area, choose whether the images should open at large size in the browser window when clicked on ("Media File" in the drop-down) or in a separate website page ("Attachment File"); you can also choose how many thumbnails

to have appearing in each gallery row, which will determine their size.

4. Click "Insert gallery" when you're done, and finally click "Update" to save the page. Now you can check how your gallery looks.

When you add the Jetpack plugin to your WordPress site (see page 75), you can implement their Carousel feature, which will make your gallery look even better—when clicked on, the images will show up within a slick side-to-side viewing system, as seen on the live demo site.

EDITING A GALLERY

To edit a gallery, click on the gallery in your editing page, then click on the button that appears at the top left, just as you would with an image.

To add an image, click "Add to Gallery" on the left-hand side and either upload further images or add them from your Media Library.

To remove an image from a gallery, click the "x" that appears at the top right of the image when you mouse over it.

Click "Update gallery" and then update the page.

You can also edit images from inside your gallery editing area. You will find this particularly useful if you find you have to rotate an image, or to create a better thumbnail picture (we'll see more about editing images in WordPress shortly). To access the editing area from inside the gallery area, click on the image you want to edit and then click the "Edit Image" link to the right-hand side of the screen.

Carry out your edit in the new browser window (see the next page), save and update, then close the browser window. Back at the gallery screen, make sure you click "Refresh" on the right-hand side (indicated) so that you can see the change that has been made. Then click "Update gallery."

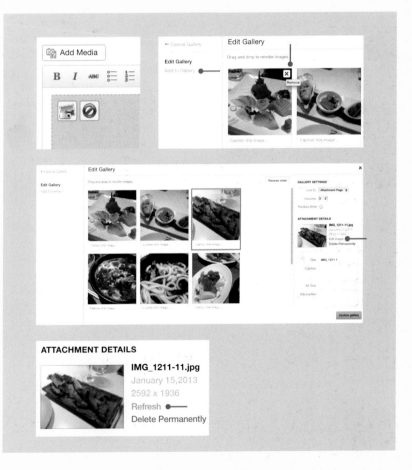

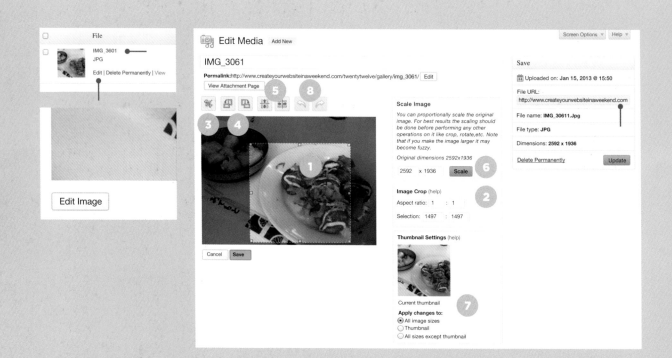

EDITING IMAGES FROM WITHIN WORDPRESS

As we have seen, WordPress has an image-editing facility that is useful for resizing and rotating images, as well as creating different thumbnail images if the ones automatically generated by the gallery don't display the image to its best advantage.

To edit an image, go to Media > Library, find your image in the list of uploaded images, and click on the image title (or use the "Edit" link that appears below it when you move your mouse over it). At this point you can change the title, caption, alt text and description, but to make changes to the image itself, click the "Edit" button underneath the image.

To crop an image, first select the area with your mouse (1). If you want this crop to be used as the thumbnail for the image, then it must be square; WordPress has a neat tool to make this easy. First, roughly select the area you want to use as the thumbnail. Then write "1" and "1" in both the boxes labeled "Aspect Ratio" (2). Click back inside the selected area with your mouse and move it slightly—you will find the selected area automatically squares itself. Move the selected area around until you're happy with the crop and when you are, click the "Crop" button (3).

You can also do the following within the editing area:
> Rotate the image (4).
> Flip the image vertically or horizontally (5).
> Resize the image keeping the same proportions (6).
> Choose the versions of the images to which the change will apply (7). This tool is often used only for thumbnails (the main image will remain the same).
> Undo your changes if necessary (8).

Click "Save," then click "Update when you're done.

Adding video and audio to YOUR SITE

VIDEO

WordPress has made adding videos to your website as easy as possible.

1. **If you want** to show your own video, open an account (free) with a video-sharing site such as YouTube or Vimeo, and upload your video there.
2. **For YouTube**, navigate to the video you want to show on your website, then click "Share" below the video, and copy the web address that appears beneath it. **For Vimeo**, simply copy the web address of the video from your browser address bar.

3. **Paste** this into your page editing box, where you want the video to appear, on a separate line of its own (as shown below).
4. **Click** "Update," and you'll see the video embedded into your site.

(This simple one-line paste also works with other video- or image-sharing sites, such as DailyMotion and Flickr.)

AUDIO

To upload audio to your site, the file must be in MP3 format.

1. **Click** in your page editing box where you want the audio link to appear.
2. **Click** the "Add Media" button as though you were uploading an image, and upload the MP3 to your Media Library.
3. **In the** "Title" field, write the text that you want people to click on to listen to the audio. Select "Media File" in the "Link to:" drop-down.
4. **Click** "Insert into page."
5. **Click** the blue "Update" button to save your page.

Your blog or NEWS AREA

Earlier on when you assigned your home page to the front page of your site, you (optionally) designated a page as your blog or news area.

If you go to that page on your live site, you can see the dummy post that WordPress puts in for you, with the title "Hello world!"

Creating and editing blog posts works in exactly the same way as creating and editing pages. The difference is that you don't have to link them to a menu. Blog posts appear automatically on the page you've designated as your blog or news page, in a long list, with the most recent post at the top of the page.

To delete the dummy post and create your own blog posts, go to Posts > All Posts.

Move your mouse over the dummy "Hello world!" title, and click "Trash" to remove it.

Now, click on "Add New," either at the top of the page or in the left-hand navigation (under "Posts" rather than "Pages"), and then type in and publish your own blog post —including any images, audio, or videos if you like, in exactly the same way you did with your site pages.

CATEGORIES AND TAGS

One feature blog posts have that pages do not is that they can be categorized into different topics of interest. The benefit of doing this is that you can add a list of your categories into the sidebar, allowing visitors to choose which blog posts they want to read, according to topic.

Although this feature is optional, if you don't choose to assign your blog posts to different categories, they will show up as having been classed as "Uncategorized," which can look clumsy. The best way around this is to change the name of the "Uncategorized" category. You could change it to "Blog" or "News," or something more specific that is suitable for your site.

Categories and subcategories can be added directly from the blog-editing page, or from the special "Categories" area of the left-hand navigation.

To assign a post to a category while you are working on it, use the "Categories" box to the right, as shown in the screenshot.

To rename the "Uncategorized" category, go to Posts > Categories. Move your mouse over "Uncategorized" and click the "Edit" link that appears underneath it. Change the category name and the slug and click "Update." (The slug is simply how the category will look as a web address. Just type the same title as you did into the "Category Name" field and WordPress will

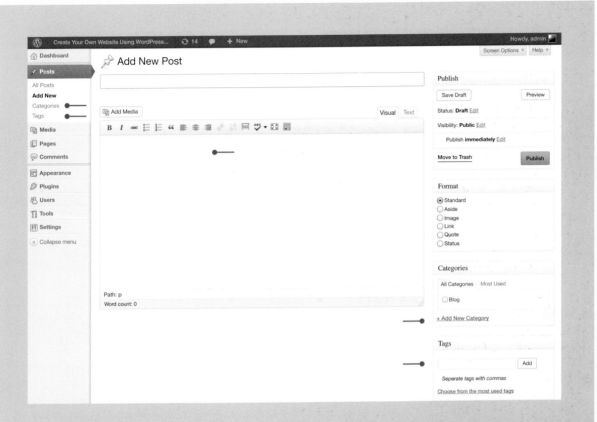

format it as it needs it.) After that, click "Update".

You can also assign "tags" to your blog posts, which is a different way of allowing people to find posts according to areas of interest. Categories are general ways of grouping posts together—filing them, if you like—whereas tags can relate more specifically to the topic of the blog post; you can consider them as keywords that relate to the subject matter of the post. Like categories, tags can be managed in their own

area, which you access from the left-hand navigation, or from the "Tags" box on the main editing page, found underneath the "Categories" box (as shown in the screenshot above).

You can show your tags in your sidebar in the form of a "tag cloud"—a group of tags of different sizes, the largest being the ones you use most.

There is no obligation to use either categories or tags—they can quite safely be ignored—but if you are going to do a lot of blogging, your readers will find them useful.

THE DIFFERENCE BETWEEN CATEGORIES AND TAGS

It can be difficult to grasp the difference between categories and tags. Here's a wardrobe metaphor that may help. You classify your clothes by type—socks, jackets, shirts, and so on; these you can consider your categories. Tags will be the way you describe the individual items of clothing—knitted, purple, woollen, silk, vintage, summer, evening.

ENABLING COMMENTS

Back in the "First Steps" section of the setup, you decided whether to have comments enabled or disabled by default; I suggested that you disable comments while creating your site pages. If you want to let your readers leave comments on your blog posts, now is the time to change the default to "Enabled," so that they are automatically enabled for each blog post you create—go to Settings > Discussion to make this change. (You can always enable comments for individual posts, but it will most likely be more convenient to enable them right across the board for your blog posts.)

To enable or disable comments manually for individual posts:

1. **Go** to the individual blog-post page and scroll down to the box entitled "Discussion." Check, or uncheck, the box next to "Allow comments."
2. **If you can't see the box,** click the "Screen Options" tab towards the top right of your screen and check the "Discussions" checkbox.
3. **You'll now be able to see** the "Discussion" box at the bottom of the page (underneath the text editing area); check or uncheck the "Allow comments" box as required.
4. **Click** the blue "Update" button to save your changes.

We will see how to enable Akismet, a plugin that protects you from comment spam, on page 74.

MAKING A POST "STICKY"

Making a post "sticky" will ensure it remains at the top of the blog page and will therefore always be visible. You might choose to do this with certain topical, or frequently read posts, or create an introduction to the blogging section of your site that you want to be sure your site visitors notice. You can make a blog post sticky either in the "Quick Edit" view from your list of blog posts, or within the "Publish" box of the main editing page. When a standard blog post is made sticky, it will show up with a "Featured Post" label above it (see opposite for info on different kinds of blog posts).

BLOG POST FORMATS

With the default theme, though not with all themes, WordPress offers you the choice of formatting your blog posts in different ways. If your blog is going to be a major feature of your site, you will want to make use of these to make your blog page as lively and varied as possible. Apart from the standard blog post, the alternative formats you have available to you are:

> Aside
> Image
> Link
> Quote
> Status

You can see how these look on the screenshot, or go to the blog page of the live demo site.

To assign a format to a post, select one of the radio buttons from the "Format" box before saving the post.

Format

- ◉ Standard
- ○ Aside
- ○ Image
- ○ Link
- ○ Quote
- ○ Status

FEATURED IMAGES

Posts can have a "featured image" added to them which will stand out more than an image inserted into the body of the post, as it will appear above the blog post heading. To add a featured image, click the "Choose a Featured Image" button from the lower right-hand side of your post editing page.

Create Your Own Website Using WordPress in a Weekend

This is the blog section of the site

Leave a reply

This is the blog section of the website. Here is where your blog or news items will go. This is an example of a "Standard" blog post. I've made it "Sticky" so that it stays at the top of the page. Any type of blog post can be made "sticky," but it's only standard-format blog posts that get the title "Featured Post" above them. I've also added a featured iamge to the post - it's only for standard-format blog posts that featured images will show up. They appear above the heading - any other images will appera below it.

This entry was posted in Blog posts on October 18, 2012.

> **This is an aside**
> This is a blog post saved with the "Aside" format. An aside is a very short blog post with a blue background so that it shows up.

October 18, 2012
Leave a reply

This is a blog post saved with the "Image" format. You can add text to an image post - perhaps to explain the image - but its title won't show up, in order not to detract from the impact of the image itself.

This is an image post
October 18, 2012
Leave a reply

This is a post saved with the "Link" format.   LINK
http://www.google.com

October 18, 2012
Leave a reply

This is a blog post saved with the "Quote" format. Its title doesn't show up. It's perfect for a line or two of text, without a distracting heading.

October 18, 2012
Leave a reply

Alannah
October 18, 2012

This is a blog post saved with the "Staus" format. It shows the name and "gravatar" of the person who wrote the post. (if you have gravatars enabled in the Settings > Discussions area of the admin).

Leave a reply

Your WIDGETS

Widgets are the little bits of content —recent posts, search boxes, etc.— that you can put in the sidebar area of your pages and, with this particular theme, in the footer of the home page.

WordPress comes with certain widgets built-in; however widgets exist to do pretty much anything, and we'll see more of these when we look at plugins in the next section.

ADDING WIDGETS TO YOUR PAGES

You will have noticed that in the sidebars of your site there are already some elements that

WordPress automatically puts in for you; we need to get rid of these, so that you can put the widgets you do want in there.

1. **Go** to Appearance > Widgets in the left-hand navigation.
2. **In the box** on the right-hand side labeled "Main Sidebar," you will see the widgets WordPress puts into your sidebar by default when you first set up your site. Drag these out of the box with your mouse so that you can start afresh. (These are standard widgets, which you can always add back in later.)
3. **Now choose** which widgets you want in your sidebar by dragging

them from the central area to the "Main Sidebar" box—you can easily reorder them with your mouse.

The best way to decide which widgets you want to show on your site is to experiment with them.

REMOVING THE SIDEBAR

With the default theme, you have the option of choosing to create pages without a sidebar, and therefore without widgets. See the live demo for an example—I have created a page entitled "Full-Width Page" to show you what this will look like. To save a page with the full-width format, go to the editing screen for that page and in the box to the right entitled "Page Attributes," choose "Full-width" from the drop-down. (This was what you did when you assigned the Front Page Template to your home page.) Save the page with the blue "Update" button, as usual. Note that if you keep your sidebar empty, the sidebar area will disappear automatically from all your blog posts and pages.

In most cases, you can change the titles of the widgets—for example, the "Archives" widget may be more useful on a business site if displayed with another title (for example, "News by Month" or "Past News Bulletins"). You can open each widget to retitle it, or to see more options, by clicking the small triangle to the right.

It's completely up to you which widgets you choose to put in your sidebar—your needs will depend on the purpose of your site. I suggest "Recent Posts"—perhaps retitled as "Latest News," to show your site is dynamic and your business is busy —and a search box if your site is large, so that visitors can search by topic or keyword. If your major focus is blogging, you may want to implement the "Archives" or "Calendar" widgets, and maybe the "Categories," "Tag Cloud," and "Recent Comments" widgets as well.

You can also add widgets to the "First Front Page Area" and "Second Front Page Area." (Open the widget areas, so that you can drag elements into them, by clicking the small triangle on the right-hand side.) These will appear at the bottom of the main text on your front page in two columns. If you leave them empty, they will not show up, so using them is entirely optional. However, it is a good way of showing additional information about you or your business on the home page, so people can see more information at a glance. Again, it is up to you what material you want to include in the home page footer, but a useful implementation might be to put some more information about you in a "Text" widget in the first (left) area, and your "Recent Posts" in the second (right) area.

We'll now move on and look at plugins; when we install the Jetpack plugin, you'll find that some other useful—not to mention fun—widgets become available.

SOCIAL MEDIA WIDGETS
We often see Facebook, Twitter, and other social media buttons in website sidebars. We'll see how you can incorporate these into your site in Chapter 9.

Main Sidebar

Archives

Title:

☐ Display as dropdown
☐ Show post counts

Delete | Close   Save

TWO VERY USEFUL WIDGETS
> The "Text" widget is very useful for writing small snippets of text, such as your telephone number or address, or for highlighting a special offer. Snippets of code can also be pasted into "Text" widgets, if you ever need to do this.

> "Custom Menu"—remember how we created a menu for the site and labeled it "Main"? You can actually create any number of menus, attach pages to them, and display them in the sidebar as additional menus using the 'Custom Menu' widget. This is useful if you have a lot of pages on your site, but don't want to clutter up the main menu with them.

Custom Menu

Title:

Select Menu: Sidebar Menu ⬍

Delete | Close   Save

The plugins YOU NEED

A plugin is a component that you can add to WordPress to make it do things that it doesn't do right out of the box. We're going to install the plugins you need to complete your website, and then it will be fully functional and ready to go.

AKISMET

Akismet is a plugin so essential that it comes bundled with WordPress. It does the very important job of stopping you getting spam, either through the "Comments" area on your blog posts or from the contact form we will set up in the next step. All you need to do is activate it by putting in a special passcode so that it can start working.

For business accounts you need to sign up for a paying account—$5 a month at the time of writing—whereas for personal sites it is free (or you pay voluntarily). Sign up for whichever is applicable to you—you really do need an Akismet account.

1. **Go** to Plugins > Installed Plugins.
2. **Find** "Akismet" at the top of the list of plugins that come ready installed, and click the "Activate" link underneath it.
3. **Click** the link that says "Sign up for an Akismet API key." (This simply functions as your passcode.)
4. **Sign** up for an Akismet key on the Akismet site, choosing the account type that is applicable to you. Check your email and copy the key they have sent you.

5. **Go** back to your plugins page and click the link that says "Go to your Akismet configuration page."
6. **Paste** the key in the field (as indicated below), and then click "Update Options."

Now that Akismet is activated, you can go to the Settings > Discussion area and uncheck the boxes next to "Before a comment appears." This means that comments will go up without you having to moderate them, but Akismet will have filtered out any that are spam. Do keep an eye on your comments in the "Comments" area on the left-hand navigation of your admin area, as very occasionally Akismet will misjudge a comment as spam when it isn't, and vice versa. But it does a very good job—if you check the "Akismet Stats" area, you'll see just how much spam it filters out.

> Monitor and reply to your comments from the "Comments" area of the admin. You'll find Akismet almost never publishes spam by mistake, but you should still keep an eye out.

3

	Plugin	Description
☐	**Akismet** Deactivate | Edit | Settings	Used by millions, Akismet is quite possibly the best way in the world to **protect your blog from comment and trackback spam**. It keeps your site protected from spam even while you sleep. To get started: 1) Click the "Activate" link to the left of this description, 2) **Sign up for an Akismet API key**, and 3) Go to your Akismet configuration page, and save your API key. Version 2.5.6 | By Automattic | Visit plugin site

6

Akismet Configuration

Akismet is almost ready. You must **enter your Akismet API key** for it to work.

For many people, Akismet will greatly reduce or even completely eliminate the comment and trackback spam you get on your site. If one does happen to get through, simply mark it as "spam" on the moderation screen and Akismet will learn from the mistakes. If you don't have an API ket yet, you can get one at Akismet.com.

Akismet API Key

Please enter an API key. (Get your key.)

_____ (What is this?)

☐ Auto-delete spam submitted on posts more than a month old.

☐ Show the number of comments you've approved beside each comment author.

[Update options »]

A CONTACT FORM VIA JETPACK

Jetpack is a plugin bundle containing many tools that were, until recently, only available for WordPress.com users. These will save you lots of time setting up individual plugins that do the same job, which is ideal for getting your site up and running in a weekend. Getting Jetpack will mean signing up for a WordPress.com account, but this is not a problem—you don't have to actually use their blogging system.

First, we'll install the Jetpack bundle, and then we'll be able to add a contact form to your contact page.

Many premium templates come with a ready-made contact form, so ultimately, you may not need this one. But it is worth installing Jetpack anyway so you can make use of the other tools it offers.

1. **Go** to Plugins > Installed Plugins.
2. **Find** "Jetpack" in the list of plugins that are already installed, and then click the "Activate" link underneath.
3. **Click** the green button labeled "Connect to WordPress.com."
4. **Click** the link that says, "Need an account?" and fill in the details.
5. **Check** your email, and click the link to activate the account. Finally, click the blue button to complete the authorization .

You'll see a new section in your left-hand navigation called "Jetpack" —click on it and you'll see a range of interesting tools the plugin offers you (see right).

To install a "Contact" form:

1. Go to your "Contact" page (Pages > All Pages > Contact).

2. Click inside the text-editing area, then click on the new button you can see next to the button you use to add images.

3. You can set up the form in whatever way suits you; however I prefer to make two changes: 1) first remove the "Website" field, as I don't think it's necessarily appropriate (not everyone writing to you will have a website)—do this by clicking on the "-" sign next to it; then 2) change the title of the "Comments" field to "Message" by moving your mouse over it so that the "Edit" link becomes visible. Click "Edit," change the label, and save the field.

4. Now click the "Email notifications" tab, and fill in subject line of the email with something like, "Message from website." This is the email that will get sent to you whenever someone contacts you from the form. You can fill in the email address field as well, if you want the email to go to a different address from the one you used when installing WordPress; leaving it blank will send messages to your original email address. (You can also check your messages in the "Feedbacks" area of the admin page.) Save the email details by clicking the blue button below entitled "Save and go back to the form builder."

5. Click the blue button, "Add this form to my post," and then save the page with the "Update" button to finish.

2

Dashboard
Jetpack
Posts
Media
Pages
All Pages
Add New
Comments
Feedbacks
Appearance

Edit Page Add New

Contact

Permalink: http://www.alannamoore.com/twentytwelve/contact/ Edit View Page Get Shortlink

Add Media

Visual Text

B I ABC ≔ ≔ " ≡ ≡ ≡

Paragraph U A ⬠ ⬚ ⬚ Ω

3

Add a custom form ✕

Form builder | Email notifications

Here's what your form will look like

Name (required)

Email (required)

Website

Comment (required)   move   edit

Add a new field

Add this form to my post

How does this work?

By adding a contact form, your readers will be able to submit feedback to you. All feedback is automatically scanned for spam, and the legitimate feedback will be emailed to you.

Can I add more fields?

Sure thing. Click here to add a new text box, textarea, radio, checkbox, or dropdown field.

Can I view my feedback within WordPress?

Yep, you can read your feedback at any time by clicking the "Feebacks" link in the admin menu.

EMAIL PROTECTOR

You now have a contact form on your contact page that makes it easy for visitors to your site to contact you via your website. However, as explained when planning your website in Chapter 3, it adds credibility to your site when people can see your real email address. If you are a blogger, this may not be an issue; however, if you have a real-world identity that your site is promoting, then it is important. The problem is that once your email address is posted on your website, spammers can "harvest" your email address. You need to protect it, and that's where the "Email Protector" plugin comes in handy.

1. **Go** to Plugins > Add New. Type "Email Protector" into the "Search" field, and click 'Search Plugins."
2. **Underneath** where you see "Pixeline's Email Protector," click "Install Now," "OK," then "Activate Plugin."
3. **Now,** go to your "Contact" page and type your email address, either above or below the form.
4. **Save** the page, and look at the live page on your site. You will now have a live email link on your site, which people can click on and send an email directly to you, but the email address will be disguised from harvesters.

(You will want to add some text to your contact page, such as "Please contact me either by email or by using the form below." As discussed in Chapter 3, whether or not you want to include your address and telephone number is up to you.)

---

①

🔌 **Install Plugins**

Search | Upload | Featured | Popular | Newest | Favorites

Plugins extend and expand the functionality of WordPress. You

Search

| email protector ⊗ | Search Plugins |

---

②

Name	Version	Rating
Pixeline's Email Protector	1,2,3	☆☆☆
Details | Install Now		
Cryptex - Email Obfuscator+Protector	2.0	☆☆☆
Details | Install Now		

---

②

🔌 **Installing Plugin: Pixeline's Email Protector 1.2.3**

Downloading install package from http://downloads.wordpress.org/plugin/pixelines-email-protector

Unpacking the package...

Installing the plugin...

Successfully installed the plugin **Pixeline's Email Protector 1.2.3.**

Activate Plugin | Return to Plugin Installer

[Activate this plugin]

SITE STATS VIA JETPACK

Once your site starts receiving visitors, tracking your traffic (how your visitors find you, which pages they visit) is essential to chart your site's progress. One of the elements that comes with Jetpack is a built-in "Site Stats" section; you can visit it by clicking Jetpack > Site Stats on the left-hand navigation.

We'll be talking more about tracking traffic in Chapter 9, where we see how you can use Google Analytics to get more detailed traffic reports than the ones provided via Jetpack.

ALL IN ONE SEO PACK

Attracting traffic through the search engines is vital to the success of your site. We will be going into how to optimize your website in further detail in Chapter 9, but in order to prepare for this, you will need to install another plugin—we'll leave its configuration until later, as some explanation is required first as to how search engines work.

1. **Go to** Plugins > Add New. Type "All in One SEO Pack" in the "Search" field, and click "Search Plugins."
2. **Underneath** "All in One SEO Pack," click "Install Now," then "OK," then "Activate Plugin."
3. **Go to** the "Admin" page by clicking on the link.
4. **For now,** just enable the plugin by selecting the radio button, and then click the blue "Update Options" button right at the bottom of the page to save.

EXTRA TOOLS IN JETPACK

You will want to explore the different tools that come with Jetpack, which can add even more life and interactivity to your site. These need to be enabled, and sometimes also configured, from within the Jetpack area of the admin.

Some of these are:

> Sharing icons (Facebook, Twitter, LinkedIn, etc.) that will appear at the bottom of selected pages and blog posts—we'll go through this when we discuss social media in Chapter 9.
> Publicize—have your blog posts appear automatically on Facebook, Twitter, or LinkedIn.
> Email subscriptions—add a sign-up form to your sidebar (this is a widget that enables people to receive blog updates by email each time you post a news post; a great way to keep in touch with your site visitors).
> Adding a Facebook Like box to your site (another widget).
> Adding a Twitter feed to your sidebar (another widget).
> Showing images in your sidebar (yet another widget).
> Optionally display your galleries as slideshows instead (inside the page).
> Image Carousel—after enabling the Carousel feature, you'll see that your galleries look much more professional: when you click on an individual image, the images are now all beautifully displayed, large-size, in a right-to-left stream. See the example on the live demo website on the page titled "Gallery."
> Tiled Galleries—alternatively, display your galleries in a mosaic layout.
> Shortcode Embeds—include SoundCloud audio clips embedded into pages.

3   🔌 **Plugins**   Add New

All in One SEO Pack must be configured. Go to the admin page to enable and configure the plugin. All in One SEO Pack now supports Custom Post Types and Google Analytics..

Plugin **activated.**

4   Plugin Status: ◉ Enabled
                    ◯ Disabled

HOW TO ADD A COPYRIGHT LINE AT THE BOTTOM OF YOUR SITE

WordPress doesn't give you an easy way of adding a copyright line when you're using the default theme, whereas many of the premium themes do. So to add one, we need to go into the code. Don't be put off—it's very easy if you just follow these steps. You won't want to do this if you're planning to work on a different theme for your real, live website. But if you are going to continue with the default theme, this will be a finishing touch.

1. **Go to** Appearance > Editor.
2. **Click** "Footer (footer.php)" from the list on the right-hand side.
3. **Look** at the code, and find the exact spot indicated by the red arrow in the screenshot to the right. (That is, directly after the "</a>".)
4. **Type:**

Copyright © 2013 Your name or business name. All rights reserved.

(Or an alternative copyright notice; the "<br>" just makes a line break.)

Your code should now look like this (4).

5. **Click** the blue "Update file" button, and check how it looks on the live site.

I think it is nice to keep the WordPress credit, since this is, after all, a free software. But if you do want to remove it, you need to delete this whole bit of code (6, highlighted in blue) and save the page.

3

```
        </div><!-- #main .wrapper -->
        <footer id="colophon" role="contentinfo">
                <div class="site-info">
                        <?php do_action( 'twentytwelve_credits' ); ?>
                        <a href="<?php echo esc_url( __( 'http://wordpress.org/',
'twentytwelve' ) ); ?>" title="<?php esc_attr_e( 'Semantic Personal Publishing Platform',
'twentytwelve' ); ?>" rel="generator"><?php printf( __( 'Proudly powered by %s',
'twentytwelve' ), 'WordPress' ); ?></a>
                </div><!-- .site-info -->
        </footer><!-- #colophon -->
</div><!-- #page -->
```

4

```
        <footer id="colophon" role="contentinfo">
                <div class="site-info">
                        <?php do_action( 'twentytwelve_credits' ); ?>
                        <a href="<?php echo esc_url( __( 'http://wordpress.org/',
'twentytwelve' ) ); ?>" title="<?php esc_attr_e( 'Semantic Personal Publishing Platform',
'twentytwelve' ); ?>" rel="generator"><?php printf( __( 'Proudly powered by %s',
'twentytwelve' ), 'WordPress' ); ?></a><br> Copyright © 2013 Alannah Moore. All rights
reserved.
                </div><!-- .site-info -->
        </footer><!-- #colophon -->
</div><!-- #page -->
```

5

Proudly powered by WordPress

Copyright © 2013 Alannah Moore. All rights reserved.

6

```
        <footer id="colophon" role="contentinfo">
                <div class="site-info">
                        <?php do_action( 'twentytwelve_credits' ); ?>
                        <a href="<?php echo esc_url( __( 'http://wordpress.org/',
'twentytwelve' ) ); ?>" title="<?php esc_attr_e( 'Semantic Personal Publishing Platform',
'twentytwelve' ); ?>" rel="generator"><?php printf( __( 'Proudly powered by %s',
'twentytwelve' ), 'WordPress' ); ?></a><br>Copyright © 2013 Alannah Moore. All rights
reserved.
                </div><!-- .site-info -->
        </footer><!-- #colophon -->
</div><!-- #page -->
```

Note that as the years pass, you will want to extend your copyright notice so that it reads *"Copyright © 2013-14 Your name or business name. All rights reserved."*—and so on.

Create Your Own Website Using WordPress in a Weekend

Demo site using the Twenty Twelve theme

HOME   ABOUT   FULL-WIDTH PAGE   **BLOG**   CONTACT

Learn to build your own website

This is a dummy website set up to accompany Chapter 5 of *Create Your Own Website Using WordPress in a Weekend*.

In this chapter of the book we see how the WordPress default theme "Twenty Twelve", released as the default theme as from December 2012, can be used to create a simple website for any kind of business or personal site, or blog.

The new default theme has a clean and fresh design and is fully responsive, meaning that it looks really good on smartphones and tablets.

WIDGET AREA

This is a useful widget area where you might choose to put more information about you on the front page, so that visitors get more information at a glance which they might otherwise miss.

RECENT BLOG POSTS

This is the blog section of the site

This is an aside

This is an image post

This is a link

This is a quote

	Search

Proudly powered by WordPress

Basic site completion CHECKLIST

Congratulations—you've now completed all the steps necessary to get your basic WordPress site up and fully functional.

You have achieved the following:

> The first steps of the website setup—such as setting your time zone, your name as it will appear on the blog, your permalinks, etc.
> Customizing the look of the site—your header text, a custom header, and changing the background color or image as required.
> Creating pages.
> Linking pages to the menu.
> Working with the text editor.
> Adding images to your site.
> Adding video and audio content, if you wanted to include these.
> Creating blog posts.
> Adding widgets to your sidebar and footer.
> Installing the essential plugins: Akismet, Jetpack, Email Protector, and the All in One SEO Pack.
> Adding a copyright notice to your site, if you wanted to include this.

LIVE DEMO
Remember that you can visit the live demo site at http://www.createyourwebsiteinaweekend.com/twentytwelve

The web world changes quickly, and constantly. Make sure you sign up for updates at http://www.createyourwebsiteinaweekend.com to be certain you're in the loop.

What Next?

What do you think of your new website? Are you happy with the way it looks? Perhaps you're looking forward to leaping into something more complex that allows you more creativity and free rein. If the latter case applies, read on.

If you're content with your basic website as it is, you can jump ahead to Chapter 9, where we'll look at what you need to know in order to manage and market your live website.

Note: If you are going to use the site you've just created as your real, live website, don't forget that you do want it to be visible in the search engines. Go back to Settings > Reading, unselect the checkbox next to "Discourage search engines from indexing this site," and save your change.

6

Selling from your website
ACCEPTING ONLINE PAYMENTS

Accepting payment online can be a complicated business involving internet merchant accounts, complex shopping carts, and payment gateways. While this may be appropriate for you further down the line, if you want to set up your website in a weekend and take payment online as easily and painlessly as possible, using PayPal as your payment processor is probably the best option.

It may take several days to get your PayPal account up and running, so hopefully, as suggested at the beginning of the book, you have been able to get everything organized in advance before starting to build your site.

You may also want to think about allowing your site visitors the additional options of mailing you a check or arranging to pay you via a bank transfer, but this will mean extra work on your part. These options should always be in addition to—not instead of—making payments via an instant, online method, which most people prefer.

Using PAYPAL

PayPal is an online payment processor that allows you to take payments from your website via a credit or debit card quickly and easily. Your purchasers can also pay with funds they have in their PayPal accounts, but they do not have to have a PayPal account to pay you with a credit card. To accept payments via PayPal, all you need to do is get an account and add a snippet of code to your web pages, which will then add a payment button—funds accumulated via PayPal can then be transferred directly to your own bank account.

There is no setup fee or monthly fee, but you will be charged a transaction fee each time you receive a card payment, and also for international "PayPal to PayPal" transactions.

To accept purchases made via PayPal on your site, you need a premier or business account; the main difference is that you can't set up a premier account using your business name.

To set up a business account, you'll need to have your business information to hand, including your business bank account details and business address (the precise details required vary from country to country). When choosing which kind of business account to use, select "Website Payments Standard" for the free standard account. There will be an approval period of a few days before you're ready to take payments;

PayPal is the easiest way of accepting payments online (http://www.paypal.com).

premier users will also have to verify their bank details. You can always upgrade to a business account at a later date if you don't have all the information you need at this stage.

Once you have your PayPal account functional, you have two options:
> Using PayPal's simple "Buy Now" or "Add to Cart" buttons, which you can then add to your site, no matter which theme you are using.
> Using a free plugin like WooCommerce or WP E-Commerce, which will enable you to use a specially designed e-commerce theme to create an online store.

The first option will be the most practical if you only have a few articles you want to collect payment for—it's also very easy. The second

option requires more concentration to set up, but will give you an entirely professional-looking e-commerce store, so you'll be ready to start selling your products in your own online "shop" within just a few hours.

On the next page, you'll learn how to add PayPal buttons to your site. In Chapter 8, we'll walk through the setup of a free e-commerce theme that uses the WooCommerce plugin.

GOOGLE CHECKOUT
Google Checkout (now merged with Google Wallet) is another quick-and-easy payment system you can use as an alternative to (or in addition to) PayPal, but your visitors will have to have a Google account to use it, or will need to sign up for one in order to make purchases.

PayPal buttons and SHOPPING CART

You can add simple "Buy Now" buttons if you're just selling a few individual articles. If you imagine your visitors making more than one purchase at a time, it makes sense to let them add their purchases to a shopping cart and pay for them in one go; in this case, choose the "Add to Cart" button instead. Both options are a snip to implement—all you need to do is add a morsel of code to your pages or posts.

Japanese cookery classes at your home

Learn how to create perfect Japanese dishes at your own home. Our classes provide a wonderful, informal way of learning the delights of Japanese cooking.

Choose from the following courses:

- Sushi and Sashimi
- Noodle dishes
- Canapes
- Dumplings
- Gourmet course - a series of six classes

Our teachers are experienced and friendly and will bring all the equipment and ingredients you need to your own home.

Invite up to six of your friends to your own personal Japanese cooking class.

Sushi & Sashimi evening

For six guests $185.00 USD

Buy Now

VISA VISA

A "Buy Now" button with a drop-down menu; see over the page to see the "Add to Cart" button and other buttons you can set up with PayPal.

HOW TO ADD PAYPAL BUTTONS TO YOUR SITE

1. **Log in** to your PayPal account. Go to "Merchant Services," then to "Website Payments Standard" underneath the "Get Started" column.

2. **Under** "Option 1: Adding buttons," click on "Create button now."

3. **Add** details of the product you are selling:

   i. Keep the drop-down menu open at the "Buy Now" option; then add in the name and price.

   ii. If you like, add the details of the different options available to the buyer, which will appear as a drop-down menu, with or without different pricing options. A text field can also be added, which may be useful for the buyer to add comments or special instructions. (Remember to click the yellow "Done" button after adding each element.)

   iii. You can also opt to change the size of the button; add credit-card logos; change the language of the button; or change the wording to "Pay Now" instead of "Buy Now."

   iv. Add postage, if needed.

   v. Under the "Step 2" set of options, add inventory details, if you wish.

   vi. Go to "Step 3" and choose various other details—such as whether or not you need the customer's postal address, if you need them to give you further special instructions, etc. Ignore the "Advanced variables" field. (See page 87 for notes on creating a "Thank You page," which you can also configure at this stage.)

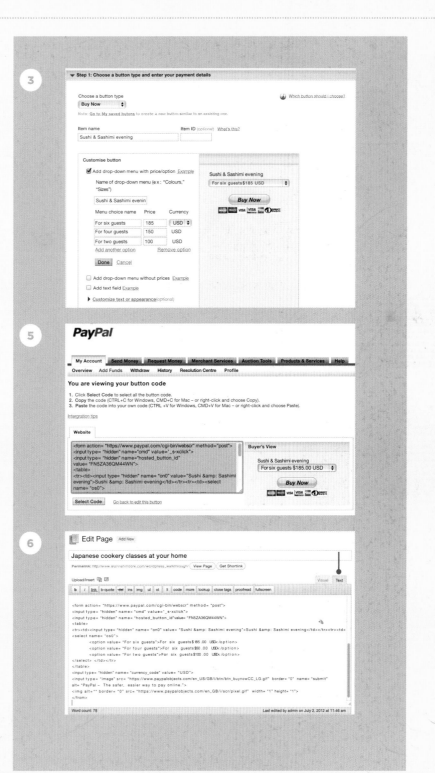

4. **Click** "Create Button" at the bottom of the page.

5. **Click** "Select Code," and then copy it (Ctrl + C for PC; Cmd + C for Mac), as shown on the previous page.

6. **Go** to your website administration area and paste the code (Ctrl + V for PC; Cmd + V for Mac) where you would like your button to appear (usually underneath a description and thumbnail-sized image of what you are selling). Use the Text view rather than the Visual view of the text-editing area, as indicated on the previous page.

7. **As usual**, save the page in your website admin by clicking the blue "Update" button.

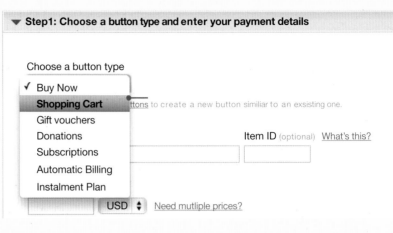

Adding "Add to Cart" buttons

To add "Add to Cart" buttons that allow your visitors to make multiple purchases at the same time, the process is identical; just choose "Shopping cart" instead of "Buy Now" when you're choosing your button type. In the same way, you can choose to create a gift voucher, "Donate" button, or any of the other options PayPal offers (see screenshot below).

TIP

PayPal saves your buttons so you can create similar ones for other products, which is a real time-saver.

Step1: Choose a button type and enter your payment details

Choose a button type

| Buy Now ⬍ |

Note: Go to My saved buttons to create a new button similiar to an exsisting one.

The different buttons, and payment types, offered by PayPal. The Steps in the column on the left offer helpful accompanying notes.

Step 1: Choosing a button	**WHAT TYPE OF BUTTONS DOES PAYPAL HAVE?**		
Step 2: Creating a button	**Buy Now**	**Add to Cart**	**Donate**
Step 3: Inserting a button	For buying just one item at a time.	For buying more than one item at a time.	For making charitable donations.
Step 4: Advanced features	Create a Buy Now button	Create an Add to Cart Button	Create a Donate button
Step 5: Testing a button	**Buy Gift Certificate**	**Subscribe**	**Automatic Billing**
	Gives customers the option of buying vouchers.	For making regular payments, such as subcriptions.	For variable monthly amounts.
	Create a Gift Voucher Button	Create a Subscribe Button	Learn more

Extra options to make the shopping experience more professional

> If you're good at using graphics software, you can create your own button instead of using the default PayPal button. Create your button and upload it to the Media Library from the administration area of your site; then copy its URL. Click the button next to "Use your own button image" and paste in the URL. Your custom button will now show up instead of the default PayPal button.

> A "Thank You" page obviously serves primarily to thank your customers after they have bought something from you, but it also lowers your charge-back rates—i.e., people asking for their money back—if you tell customers precisely what to expect after they've made the purchase. So, on your "Thank You" page, after thanking the customer for making the purchase, you should write something like: "We will contact you within 24 hours to confirm we have received your order, and will confirm delivery dates with you. In the meantime, if you have any questions, please do not hesitate to call us on xxx, or email us at this address: xxx, and we will respond to you as soon as we can." This should deter them from canceling their order if they don't hear back from you instantly!

▼ <u>Customize text or appearance</u>(optional)

● PayPal button

☑ Use smaller button

☐ Display debit and credit card logos

Country and language for button

United Kingdom - English ▲▼

Select button text

Buy Now ▲▼

○ Use your own button image
What's this?

☑ Take customers to this URL when they finish checkout

[●——]

Example:https://www.mystore.com/success

To create a "Thank You" page, first create a page within the admin area, and then give it a title using something like "Thank you for your purchase." Preview the page and copy its URL, then paste it into the field in Step 3 of PayPal's button configuration process, which you can see labeled "Take customers to this URL when they finish checkout." Then, after customers have made their purchase, they will get directed immediately to the "Thank You" page that you've just created.

Note that PayPal will log you out of your session surprisingly quickly for security reasons, so you'll need to have these elements ready before you start working on your buttons, otherwise you may find yourself automatically logged out and have to start again.

7

Exploring themes
CHOOSING HOW TO DISPLAY YOUR CONTENT

The content of your site may be what's really important, but it is the theme that will bring it to life and create the image of your site—and you or your business—that the world will see.

The theme controls not only the "look" of your site —its colors, font, background, and so forth— but also the way the information is displayed: what you include on your front page; whether you use images in your header panel to bring home the importance of your selling points; and so on. So, it is essential that you choose the right theme in order to create the best impression and convey your message effectively.

The stunning quality of the themes available— and the sheer quantity of them—is one of the joys of building your own website using WordPress; however, choosing exactly which one to use can be challenging.

Free or PREMIUM?

There are thousands of WordPress themes available that can be downloaded and installed in a matter of seconds. Many are free, but many of the most mouth-watering ones you will find you have to pay for.

The price of a commercial paid-for theme is remarkably low, usually ranging from about $30–$97 at the top end of the scale, which seems to be an incredible bargain compared to what you'd pay a web designer to build a site. However, paying for a theme will not be everyone's choice; if your site is a bit of an experiment, or you're just starting out, you may not have enough in your budget for a premium theme.

Furthermore, it may not be just the budget that determines your choice —you should also consider the following:

> Free themes don't offer technical support, whereas premium ones do—and you'll most likely get free upgrades with a theme that you've paid for.

> Premium themes can usually be customized to a greater extent than free themes. Although some of the free themes are also highly customizable, don't expect them all to be so.

Don't despair if you have no budget for a premium theme. There are some great free themes out there and we'll look at several of them.

If you purchase a premium theme, be aware that there will be other people out there using the same theme as you. It is unlikely that it will be recognized once your content is in place and you have added your own logo, changed the background, and so on, but this may be an issue for you. Even if you buy exclusive rights to the theme, don't forget that others may have purchased it before you, and are entitled to keep using it.

In a nutshell: anyone can design a theme and make it available for download, so there is no guarantee of the quality of a theme if you are not paying for it. While there are some excellent free themes out there, generally speaking, if you want top-quality and technical support when you need it, you will probably have to pay for it.

A free theme: "Bizz" from WPExplorer http://www.wpexplorer.com/bizz-wordpress-theme.

A premium theme: "Impact," also from WPExplorer http://themeforest.net/ item/impact-responsive-multipurpose-theme/3674867.

Two themes by the same theme author— both are business themes with a built-in portfolio, but the premium theme offers many more options.

How to choose A THEME

The vast number of themes out there can make choosing the right theme for your website bewildering.

Here are some guidelines to help you.

> Is the theme going to fit with what you actually need? For example, if you're going to create a business-type site that will be mostly text-based, don't be seduced into choosing a beautiful-looking theme that is designed primarily to showcase images—no matter how gorgeous it looks.
> Will it display your content as you want it to be displayed? Don't let the theme layout determine how you arrange your content. You need to display your message and the rest of your content in the most suitable way for *your* website and *your* business.
> How customizable is it, and how customizable do you need it to be? The more recent premium themes tend to be more customizable, but don't assume they are—read the descriptions carefully.
> How much control does the theme allow you to have? If you don't want the content displayed as it is on the theme-demo home page, check that you have control, or the degree of control you need, over the home page layout. (This may be described as a "drag-and-drop homepage builder," or more vaguely as "multiple home-page layouts.")

Other items to check for are:
> availability of different color schemes, preferably unlimited
> multiple sidebars—allowing you to create different sidebar content for different pages (This can always be done via a plugin, but you want to make it as straightforward as possible.)
> the option to upload your own logo (You might think this may be obvious, but many free themes don't allow for this.)

Before you make maximum customizability a criterion, ask yourself which options you actually need. Many slightly older, and most free themes, may not offer a great level of customization, but may be perfect for your needs as they are.

Some other aspects to consider:
> Is it "responsive"? If a theme is responsive, that means its format will adapt to fit a cell phone. This is not an absolute necessity, although it is a current (and probably lasting) trend. If in any doubt, check it out on your cell phone to see if the theme is legible. It may be that you don't actually need a responsive theme.
> Do you want to run ads on your site? Some themes do allow spaces for ads. If there is no specific ad space allocated on your theme, you will still be able to add ads in your sidebar as widgets.

THEMES IN USE ON LIVE SITES:

Becky's Blissful Bakery is using "Boutique Theme" from Elegant Themes (http://www.beckysblissfulbakery.com).

Harley-Davidson in Barcelona is using "Natural Theme" from Organic Themes (http://www.espaciohd.com).

Nina's Cakes is using "Wootique Theme" from Woo Themes (http://www.ninascakes.es).

Le Flamant Rouge is using "Health & Beauty" from Organic Themes (http://www.leflamantrouge.se).

TIP

Customization options—and the language used to describe them—aren't standardized. If in doubt about any options, ask first—many theme sites have a forum or comments area where you can post any pre-sales queries.

Bun Mee is using "Restaurant Theme" from Organic Themes (http://www.bunmee.co).

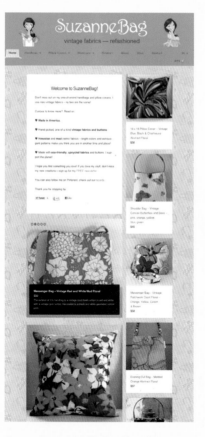

Suzanne Bag is using "Sentient Theme" from Woo Themes (http://www.suzannebag.com).

Oh My Veggies is using "Innov8tive Theme" by Studio Press (http://www.ohmyveggies.com).

Growing Book by Book is using "Going Green" by Studio Press (http://www.growingbookbybook.com).

Where to find THEMES

The WordPress Free Themes Directory (*http://wordpress.org/extend/themes*)—tied in with the "install themes" area in your site admin—is the obvious place to start looking for free themes. Here are some other places to look for both free and premium themes:

The WordPress Commercial Themes Directory (premium)
http://wordpress.org/extend/themes/commercial

WordPress Themes Base (free)
http://wordpressthemesbase.com

WP Daddy (free)
http://www.wpdaddy.com

Site 5 Themes (free)
http://www.s5themes.com

Free WP Themes (free)
http://www.freewpthemes.net

WPSkins (free)
http://www.wpskins.org

WP Templates (free; portal)
http://wptemplates.org

**WP Shower
(some free; mostly portfolio and magazine styles)**
http://wpshower.com

**Dessign (some free;
mostly portfolio and magazine)**
http://www.dessign.net

Shaken & Stirred (some free)
http://shakenandstirredweb.com

Templatic (some free)
http://templatic.com

**SkinPress
(many free; mostly blog-/magazine-type layouts)**
http://www.skinpress.com

StudioPress (premium)
http://www.studiopress.com

ThemeForest (premium)
http://themeforest.net

Elegant Themes (premium)
http://www.elegantthemes.com

WooThemes (premium)
http://www.woothemes.com

iThemes (premium)
http://ithemes.com

Templatic (premium)
http://templatic.com

Press 75 (premium)
http://press75.com

Organic Themes (premium)
http://www.organicthemes.com

Mojo Themes (premium)
http://www.mojo-themes.com

Theme Trust (premium)
http://themetrust.com

The Theme Foundry (premium)
http://thethemefoundry.com

Graph Paper Press (premium)
http://graphpaperpress.com

Obox
http://www.obox-design.com

WP Zoom (premium)
http://www.wpzoom.com

WP Now (premium)
http://www.wpnow.com

FrogsThemes (premium)
http://www.frogsthemes.com

Theme Junkie (premium)
http://www.theme-junkie.com

Template Lite
http://www.templatelite.com

This isn't an exhaustive list. Once you start looking, you'll find dozens and dozens of sites out there providing WordPress themes. If you're feeling overwhelmed, you might find the examples on the next few pages a good starting point.

Themeforest.net—source of thousands of templates created by independent designers.

Woo Themes—stunning themes created by a group of talented designers.

How to install a THEME

Themes are installed inside the "Appearance > Themes" area of the admin area.

WordPress comes with a number of free themes that are already installed, which you can see in the "Manage Themes" tab.

The handy new "Live Preview" feature (indicated right) allows you to test out how a theme will look with your own content before activating it. To activate a theme directly, click the "Activate" link.

You can add additional free themes directly from the WordPress Free Themes Directory inside the "Install Themes" area (click the tab towards the top of the page)—you can search for themes by color or other features, or if you've already chosen the theme you want to use, you can just search for it by name.

To install a premium theme, or a free theme from another source:

1. **Download** the theme from the theme website. If you're using a Mac, your computer will unzip it for you, but to upload a theme, you need it to be zipped, so you'll have to zip it again (right-click on the folder, then choose "Compress").
2. **Go** to the "Install Themes" area and click the "Upload" link.
3. **Click** "Choose File," navigate to the zip file; click "Install Now".
4. **Click** the "Live Preview Link."
5. **You** can make some basic setup changes here—click "Save and Activate" when you're done (you can customize the theme fully once it is activated).

TIP

Some theme sites will bundle an instruction manual in the same zip file as the theme. Be careful not to upload the zip file with the manual, as your theme will not work properly. Check inside the zip file first to see if there is another zip file inside—if so, this is the file you will need to upload.

You can search the WordPress Free Themes directory directly from inside your admin area.

The "Live Preview" feature allows you to try out the themes before activating them.

Themes: BUSINESS

The themes shown on the following pages show you a selection of themes designed for each of the four "kinds" of website we look at in this book. They're the tip of the iceberg, but a good starting point.

Drag & Drop
PageLines is a drag & drop framework that allows you to completely customize your website with drag & drop.

Responsive & Mobile
Built from the ground up to look great on mobile devices. PageLines utilizes an advanced responsive framework.

Tons of Addons
Load up your own sections, themes and plugins using PageLines' one of a kind extension marketplace.

PAGELINES (LITE) THEME*
(free, with premium add-on options)
from PageLines
(see Chapter 8 for demo)
http://www.pagelines.com
Install from the WordPress Free Themes Directory

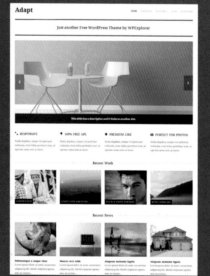

BEST (free)
from BlogEx
http://bloggingexperiment.com/best-theme

ADAPT (free)
from WPExplorer
http://www.wpexplorer.com/adapt-free-responsive-wordpress-theme

BLACKBIRD (free) from Ink Themes
http://www.inkthemes.com/wp-themes/blackbird-responsive-wordpress-theme. Install from the WordPress Free Themes Directory.

*The themes marked with an asterisk are extremely customizable. These themes can be customized to suit any kind of business, and can be changed dramatically in style and layout.

U-DESIGN* (premium)
from internq7 (ThemeForest)
http://themeforest.net/item/udesign-wordpress-theme/253220

MODERNIZE* (premium)
from GoodLayers (ThemeForest)
http://themeforest.net/item/modernize-flexibility-of-wordpress/1264247

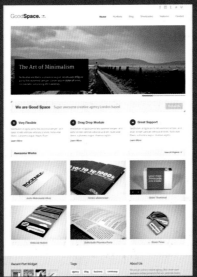

GOOD SPACE* (premium)
from GoodLayers (ThemeForest)
http://themeforest.net/item/good-space-responsive-minimal-wp-theme-/2278615

ASSOCIATE (premium)
from StudioPress
http://www.studiopress.com

Themes: **PORTFOLIO**

VISUAL THEME (free)

from Dessign (see Chapter 8 for demo)
http://www.dessign.net/visual-wordpress-theme

PORTFOLIUM (free)
from WP Shower
http://wpshower.com/themes/portfolium

IMBALANCE (free)
from WP Shower
http://wpshower.com/themes/imbalance

SHAKEN GRID (free and premium versions) from Shaken & Stirred
http://shakenandstirredweb.com

STUDIO 8 (premium) from UDFrance
http://udthemes.com/studio8-wordpress-themes

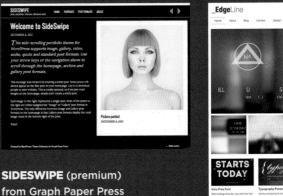

SIDESWIPE (premium)
from Graph Paper Press
http://graphpaperpress.com/themes/
sideswipe

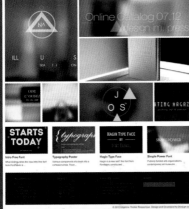

EDGELINE (premium)
from Dessign
http://www.dessign.net/edgeline-
theme-responsive

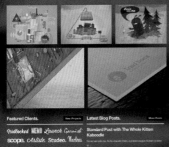

VOLUMES (premium)
from Themezilla (ThemeForest)
http://themeforest.net/item/
volumes-responsive-portfolio-
wordpress-theme/2311911

Themes: MAGAZINE/BLOG

STUCTURE (free and premium versions)
from Organic Themes (see Chapter 8
for demo of free version)
http://www.organicthemes.com

RESPO (free)
from Themnific
http://themnific.com/respo-theme

PARAGRAMS (free)
from WP Shower
*http://wpshower.com/themes/
paragrams*

UNSPOKEN (premium)
from WP Shower
*http://wpshower.com/themes/
unspoken*

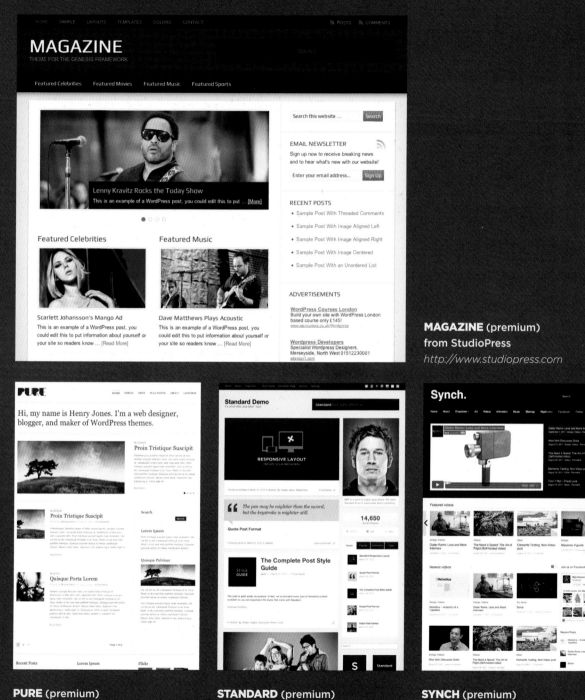

MAGAZINE (premium)
from StudioPress
http://www.studiopress.com

PURE (premium)
from ThemeTrust
http://themetrust.com/themes/pure

STANDARD (premium)
from 8Bit
http://standardtheme.com

SYNCH (premium)
from WP Shower
http://wpshower.com/themes/synch

Themes: E-COMMERCE

SLIDING (premium)
from WooThemes
http://www.woothemes.com/2011/12/sliding

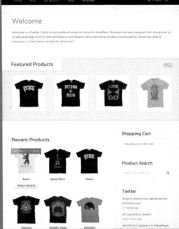

MYSTILE (free)
from WooThemes
(see Chapter 8 for demo)
http://www.woothemes.om/2012/08/
mystile

WOOTIQUE (free)
from WooThemes
http://www.woothemes.
com/2011/09/wootique

HANDMADE TWO (premium)
from Obox (ThemeForest)
http://themeforest.net/item/
handmade-two-ecommerce-
wordpress-theme/4062864

FLEXISHOP 2 (premium)
from PrimaThemes (ThemeForest)
http://themeforest.net/item/
wp-flexishop-2-a-flexible-
woocommerce-theme/2080989

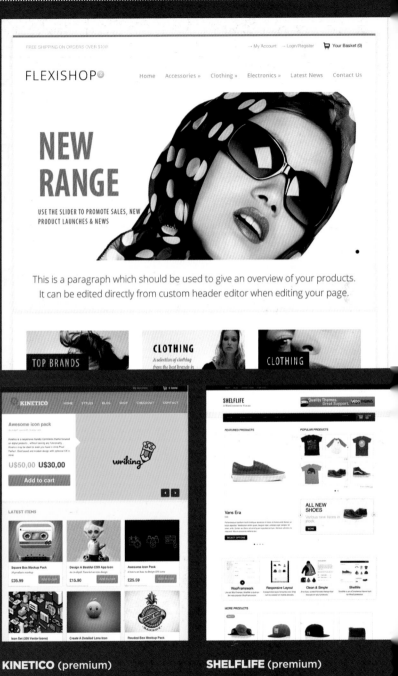

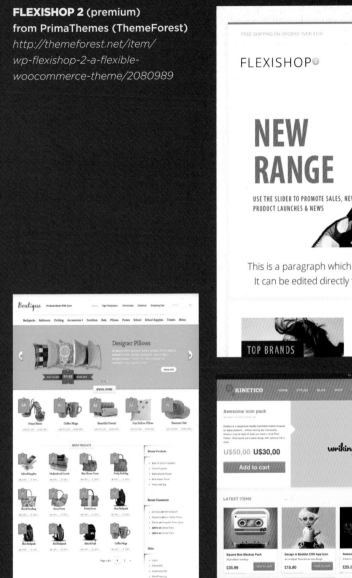

BOUTIQUE (premium)
from Elegant Themes
http://www.elegantthemes.com/
gallery/boutique

KINETICO (premium)
from RDever (ThemeForest)
http://themeforest.net/item/kinetico-
responsive-wordpress-ecommerce
/2655335

SHELFLIFE (premium)
from WooThemes
http://www.woothemes.com/2012/01/
shelflife

8

In focus

FOUR THEMES FOR FOUR TYPES OF SITE

Now that we've had a look at some of the themes available, we're going to focus on one theme for each of the "types" of website we are looking at in this book—business, portfolio, magazine, and e-commerce. For each of the chosen themes, I'll walk you through the steps necessary to set up and customize it to suit your own needs.

Business THEME

"PAGELINES" (LITE) THEME
(free, with premium add-on options) by PageLines
http://www.pagelines.com
The theme is listed in the WordPress Free Themes Directory, so it can be installed directly from inside the admin area of your website.

I've chosen this theme for the business section because of its amazing flexibility—it can be customized to suit absolutely any kind of business. You will see that you can purchase add-ons to increase the theme's functionality, however this walkthrough will use only the elements that you are provided with when you install the theme.

Adventurous readers will relish the high degree of customization possible and will be able to allow their creativity full rein when working with this theme. Less technically savvy readers may feel confused when they see the sheer amount of options available inside the admin area. Do not be dismayed, however; the walkthrough will lead you step-by-step through the customization of the theme, allowing you to create a site just like the one in the demo, and leaving experimentation to those who feel like an extra challenge.

See the functioning demo of this theme at
http://www.createyourwebsiteinaweekend.com/pagelines

This theme can be translated into any language using the Codestyling Localization plugin—see page 152.

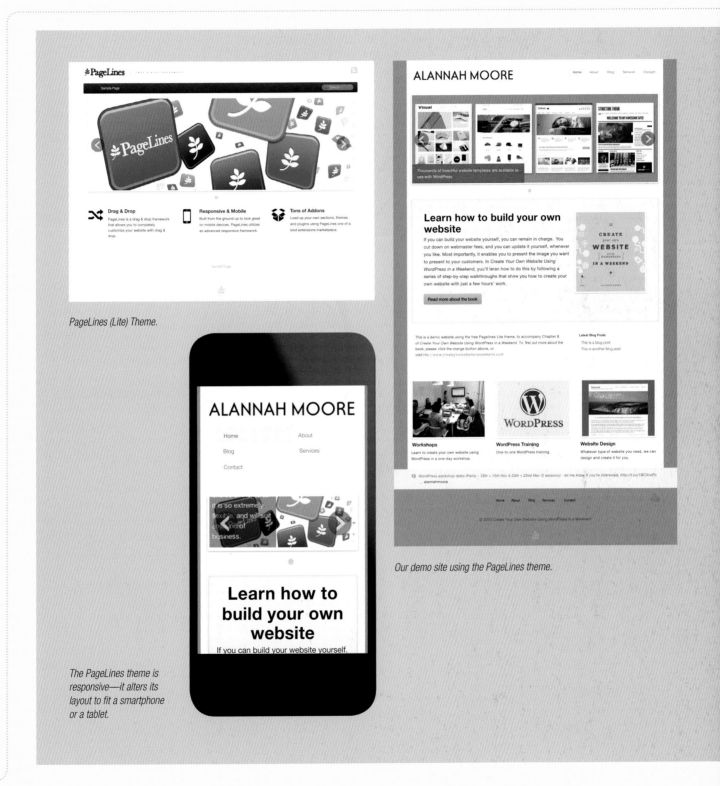

PageLines (Lite) Theme.

Our demo site using the PageLines theme.

The PageLines theme is responsive—it alters its layout to fit a smartphone or a tablet.

If you're not using a logo, I suggest you create an image file of your name or business name written in a font of your choice, and use it instead of a logo—you can use Pixlr for this. If you remove the "PageLines" logo and don't replace it with anything, your site title will show up as text in this space, looking considerably less smart and professional. Make sure the background color of the file you create matches the color you choose for your "Content Background"—I've chosen white in the demo.

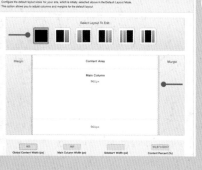

HOW TO SET UP AND CUSTOMIZE THE THEME (AS IN THE DEMO)

(see http://www.createyour websiteinaweekend.com/pagelines)

1. **Install** the theme at Appearance > Themes > Install Themes. Search "PageLines," then click "Install Now," and then "Activate."
2. **Just** as we did in the "First Steps" section for the default site (see page 37), adjust your site title and tagline if necessary, choose your time zone, check your comments and search engine settings, choose your display name for blog posts, and set your permalinks.
3. **Now**, you can begin customizing. The first thing to do is to upload your own logo to the site. Go to PageLines > Site Options. Underneath "Custom Logo" click "Upload Image" and select your logo from your computer. While you're on this page, scroll down a little and uncheck "Automatically show page titles?", before going down to the bottom of the page and clicking the blue "Save Options" button.
4. **Go to** "Layout Editor," the second item on the "Site Options" menu, underneath "Website Setup."

Scroll down the page a little to where you see "Layout Dimension Editor." Select the first layout on the left from the row of options, which gives you a single, wide column. Then, drag the side of the content area so that its width is 960. Click the blue "Save Options" button at the bottom of the page.

5. **Go to** "Color Control" from the inner menu. Here is where you

choose the colors for your background, etc. For the demo site, I have chosen a light gray "Body Background," left the "Page Background" blank, and selected white for my "Content Background." I've also chosen to change the color of my links from blue to orange, and I've darkened the footer text so that it is visible against the light gray of the background. (It may be useful to remember that #FFFFFF is the hex code for white, if you want to use this for your "Content Background".)

If you are planning to use an image for the background of the site, you can upload it through the "Site Background Image" area just underneath the color picker section; if you're using a photo, you will need to keep the checkbox next to "Supersize the Background Image" selected, so that the image will resize when viewed on a small screen or a smartphone (otherwise just a very small portion of the photo will be visible). You will also need to specify a solid "Content Background" color, to ensure the text is readable (it will be difficult for site visitors to read your text if it is displayed directly onto your image background).

Save the page when you're done.

6. Go to "Typography" from the left-hand menu. Here's where you can choose from a variety of fonts; for the demo site, I have changed the fonts from Helvetica to Arial, but you may not wish to make any changes. Save the page if you've made any alterations.

7. Go to "Header and Footer." Check "Enable Drop Down Navigation" and save.

8. You may already have your pages in place from the default demo setup. If so, you can go straight to Step 9, after making sure your home, and (optionally) your blog page, are set up as below. If you have no website content as yet, follow these steps.

In Pages > Add New, create the pages you want for your website, including a page entitled "Home." You don't need to complete the content of these pages yet—for this step, we just need them to exist on the site. Make sure you create a blog or news page at this stage, if you want one—you don't need to write anything here, just as in the default demo setup, as the system will put your blog posts on this page automatically. While you're in the Pages area, you can delete the "Sample Page" that WordPress put in for you.

Now, in Settings > Reading, in the section labeled "Front page displays," select the radio button next to "A static page," and choose the Home page from the drop-down. If you're going to have a blog section on your site, set the "Posts page" drop-down to your blog or news page. If you don't want a blog page, leave this

drop-down the way it is. Click the blue button to save the settings.

9. Go to the editing page for your home page, and from the drop-down on the right-hand side headed "Template," select "Template 1." Click the blue "Update" button. (This step will become clear, shortly.)

10. The next thing to do is set up your menu as you will need it for the next step. Go to Appearance > Menus and create a menu entitled Main. You may already have a menu ready, from the demo setup, which is perfect. When you have your menu in place with your pages in the order you want, assign the Main menu to each of the various menu positions in the box on the left entitled "Theme Locations" (these represent different menu choices but it is easiest simply to assign "Main" to them all at this stage).

11. In step 9 we assigned a layout entitled "Template 1" to the home page; we're now going to determine how that template is going to look.

Go to PageLines > Drag & Drop from the left-hand navigation. You can see that the header area (indicated in the screenshot) is colored blue, which means we are editing the header area of the home page. You have a few different options here regarding the layout of your logo and your menu. For my demo site, I have chosen the "BrandNav" layout which puts my logo to the left and the menu to the right—this suits my site, as there are just a small number of menu items. If you have a larger

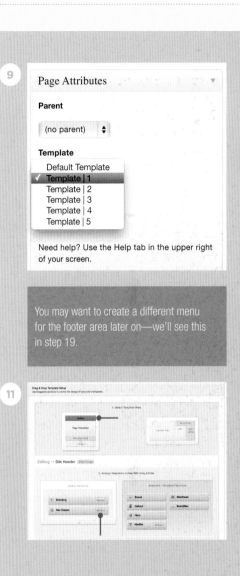

number of menu items, this won't be suitable; instead, choose either:

a. The "Branding" with "Nav Classic" option—that is, your logo with a light grey menu underneath it that looks like mine, but extends the width of the site, or:

b. The "Branding" with "NavBar" option—that is, your logo with a solid menu bar underneath it, for which you will be able to choose from several color options; blue, black, orange, etc.

To make your choice, simply drag the items you need from the right-hand box into the "Active Sections" box, and remove any that you don't want from the "Active Sections" box. (The selection being made in the screenshot is the one corresponding to Option a above.)

If you have chosen Option b, now go to PageLines > Site Options > NavBar and choose the color option you prefer. (Make your selection from the "Standard NavBar" drop-down, as shown in the screenshot—the fixed menu bar option is not available for the free version of the theme.)

The default setting for the menu bar is to include a search box on the right. If you want to remove this, scroll a little further down the page until you see a checkbox labeled "Standard NavBar—Hide Searchform?" and check the box. Click "Save Options" and see how your new menu bar now looks.

12. Now that you have your menu looking the way you want it, we are going to continue customizing

the home page. Go back to the PageLines > Drag & Drop page. Click "Page Templates" (as shown in the screenshot bottom left) and underneath it, select "Template 1" from the area entitled "For Which Type of Page?"

Drag "Quickslider" into the "Active Sections" box so that you have three elements in the "Active Sections" box; you may also, optionally, choose to add the "Hero" element, most likely underneath the Quickslider, which I'll talk about in a moment. Your selection should look as it does in the screenshot at bottom left, with or without the "Hero" element.

13. Fill in your home page content on the home page editing page, if you don't yet have any content there. (Your home page content will show up where you can see the text written on the plain white background on the demo site.) Save the page, and look at your home page on your live site; you can now see your text there.

14. We now need to put some images into our slider; go to PageLines > Page Options and click the "Quickslider" box under "Site Defaults." Here, you can configure the number of images you want to show in the slider, and a number of other settings, such as including an arrow, setting the slider to transition automatically, and so on.

At the bottom is the area where you upload the images; you will need them all to be the same height. You can size them to any dimensions you like, but a suggested size is 930 x 320. The easiest way of resizing your images is to upload them to the Media Library, scale to 930 width, crop to 930 x 320, and save. Then add them to the slider using the "Select from Library" button. (If your slider images are already the desired size, you can upload them directly to the slider area using the blue "Upload Image" button, as shown in the screenshot at right.)

As you can see, you can choose to add text to your slider images and choose the position of this text, and, if you like, link the slider images to pages on your site.

Note: If you can't see as many places to upload slides as you have specified, click "Save Options" and they will become visible.

Click "Save Options" when you have finished configuring your slider.

15. **The "Hero"** element is the boxed-out area you can see on the live demo site where I talk about this book and show the cover. Including this section won't be suitable for all kinds of business, but for some, it will be the ideal way to showcase a special offer or event, and you can even, optionally, include a striking button to make your special content really stand out.

If you want to use this element, you can configure it in the PageLines > Page Options > Site Defaults area, as you did for the slider; click on the "Hero Unit" box instead. When you have finished inputting your content and choosing how you'd

like it displayed, click the blue button to save your settings.

16. **Now** let's look at the boxes at the bottom of your home page. These are a great way of drawing attention to the services your business offers; you don't need to have just three, you can have as many or as few as you like. Create your boxes by going to Boxes > Add New Box. You can add images, and link the boxes to certain pages, a little lower down the box content editing page.

Note that as with the slider images, you will need your box images to be the same height, so that they look neat on the page (the system will automatically take care of the width). The easiest way of doing this is to choose a size for them all and scale and crop them to this size from within the Media Library (I sized mine to 600 x 448 px). When you have added an image to a box, click the "Save Meta Settings" button.

Next, select the "default-boxes" checkbox in the "Box Sets" area just below the blue "Publish" button, and then click "Publish." When you have created your boxes, delete the example boxes from the Boxes > Boxes area.

Now, go to PageLines > Page Options > Site Defaults area; click on the "Boxes" box. Here is where you can configure your boxes as you'd like them to appear. I've set mine to have the image appear on top, with the image size at 280 px, with a frame, ordered by Date, in ascending order. Save your settings when finished.

17. **The** last part of the page layout that we need to set up is the footer area. Click PageLines > Drag & Drop and then select the footer area of the template; drag the "TwitterBar" and "Footer Columns Sidebar" elements into the "Active Sections" box. (You may, or may not, want to include the "TwitterBar;" we will talk more about Social Media in Chapter 9, so don't worry if you're unsure at this stage if this will be appropriate for you.)

19

The bottom menu may be useful to include links such as Privacy and Terms & Conditions, that you do not necessarily want added to the main menu at the top of the page. To set up a separate menu for the bottom area, create the pages you want to appear in it, then create a menu entitled "Bottom" (in the Appearance > Menus area), add the new pages to the "Bottom" menu, and assign it to the "SimpleNav" section on the left on the Menus page.

20

Adding an image to a blog post via the "Featured Image" box will show a thumbnail image next to the blog post on the main blog page.

18. **If** you've added the "TwitterBar," go to PageLines > Site Options > Website Setup and scroll down until you see the area entitled "Twitter Integration." Type your Twitter username into the field labeled "Your Twitter Username" and save the setting.

19. **Go to** PageLines > Site Options > Header And Footer. Where you see "Select Number of Footer Columns," choose 1, and save the setting. Now go to Appearance > Widgets. Drag a Text widget into the "Footer Columns Sidebar" and write your copyright notice in it. I chose to center my text so that on the live site it is dislayed nicely centered in the middle of the web page, aligned with the menu elements; this you can do by typing "<center>" before the copyright notice and "</center>" after it, as shown in the screenshot.

20. **Now** that we have configured the layout of the home page, we also need to configure the layout of the blog page. If you look at your blog page now, you will see a mini version of your front page slider appearing at the top of your blog posts. If you are happy with this, you can skip this step; if not, go to PageLines > Drag & Drop. Click "Content Area" then "Blog" and remove the "Quickslider" from the "Active Sections" box, as shown in the screenshot.

21. **Now**, add some widgets to the "Primary Sidebar." These will appear on your home page and on your blog and other pages.

22. **The** penultimate step is to install your essential plugins as we did for the demo site (see page 74).

23. **Now**, all that's left to do is to arrange your page content the way you want it, and to add some blog posts to the site. You're ready to go!

When entering your page content, remember that we have configured the settings so as not to have page titles appearing automatically—this is to prevent "Home" or other text appearing very prominently on the front page, which would not suit the layout. You will need to create a page heading for each page from within the content box.

You've seen that the PageLines theme offers you many different options. If your appetite has been whetted, then there is plenty more customization you can dive into, but you may be happy with your new business site the way you have set it up.

Portfolio THEME

DEMO: "VISUAL" THEME (free)
by Marios Lublinski of Dessign.net
http://www.dessign.net/visual-wordpress-theme

A beautiful, clean, minimal portfolio layout suitable for graphic designers, photographers, artists, architects, and all creative professionals who need to display their work online.

This theme is not responsive but the layout works well on a tablet or smartphone.

You can view the functioning demo of this theme at: http://www.createyourwebsiteinaweekend.com/visual

This theme can be used for a website in any language. All you need to do is install your own language version of WordPress—see page 152.

"Visual" theme by Marios Lublinski of Dessign.net.

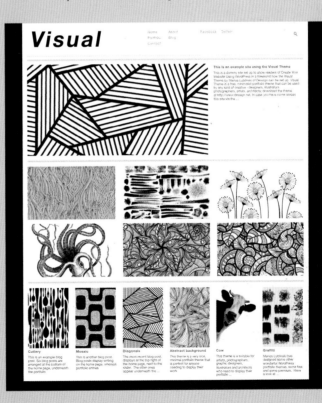

Our demo site using the "Visual" theme.

HOW TO SET UP AND CUSTOMIZE THE THEME

1. **Download** the theme from the Dessign website. If you are working on a Mac, your computer will unzip the theme for you; however, you do need it to be zipped, so zip it again by right-clicking on the "Visual Theme" folder and choosing "Compress Visual Theme."

2. **Upload** the theme by going to Appearance > Themes > Install Themes > Upload, in your admin area. Click "Choose File," select the zip file, click "Install Now," and then "Activate."

3. **When** you've uploaded the theme, you'll see a link entitled "Customize," however, it's best to go straight into the main admin area, as there you can do everything you need to do at once. So, click Appearance > Visual Settings from the left-hand navigation.

4. **Your logo** needs to be on a white (or transparent) background, and should be sized to 350 x 75 px. You can do the resizing outside WordPress, or within it—either way, you will need to upload your logo to the "Media Library" and copy its URL (web address).

The URL of an uploaded image is visible in the URL field once you have uploaded the image into the "Media Library." Scroll your mouse over the space underneath the name of the image in the "Media Library," and "Edit" will appear; click on this, and you will see the "File URL" field to the right of the image on the next screen. You can copy the web address of the image from here. Back in the "Visual Settings" area, paste the URL into the "Custom Logo URL" field.

5. **In the** "Custom Background Color" field, you can type the hex number (color code) of the color you'd like to use as a background color for the site.

You can use Pixlr to bring up a color wheel, from which you can then choose your color.

To do this, go to http://www.Pixlr.com and create a new image. Click the large rectangle at the bottom of the toolbar to the left; you can then use the color wheel that opens up to select the color for your site. Copy the six-digit/letter color code from the right-hand side of the color window; paste it into the "Custom Background Color" field in the administration area of your website.

When finished, click "Save Changes."

6. **Before** you go any further, follow the preliminary steps to set up your website exactly as we did earlier for the demo site: within the "Settings" area, set the title, date, and time; choose your search engine visibility, comments, and naming preferences; and select "Post name" for your permalinks.

7. **You** can now create the pages you want on your site.

Create your regular pages, such as your "About" and "Contact" pages, and assign the default layout to those pages. You will also need to create a "Portfolio" page and assign the portfolio layout to it, as well as a "Blog" page, to which you will assign the blog layout. (There is no need to create a "Home" page.)

Page layouts are assigned in the "Page Attributes" box to the lower right of the page-editing screen, as shown in the screenshot at right.

You do not need to perfect your pages at this stage; you can always come back to them when your setup is complete. The blog and portfolio pages are created automatically by the theme, so you don't need to do anything else to set these up.

8. **The next thing** is to link your pages to the menu so that the links appear at the top of the web page. Go to Appearance > Menus and create a new menu called "header_menu."

9. **Add** the pages you've just created to the menu from the "Pages" box (a little further down the Menus page, and to the left).

Create a "Home" link in the "Custom Links" box (above the "Pages" box), putting your domain name in the URL field, and "Home" in the "Label" field. The theme will automatically generate a home page for you, which is why you don't need to create one and add it to the menu.

Reorder the menu items by dragging them into the right position, and click "Save Menu."

10. **You** now need to create a second menu, which is for your social media links. If you don't have these in place yet, don't worry—you can always come back and complete this section once you have read Chapter 9.

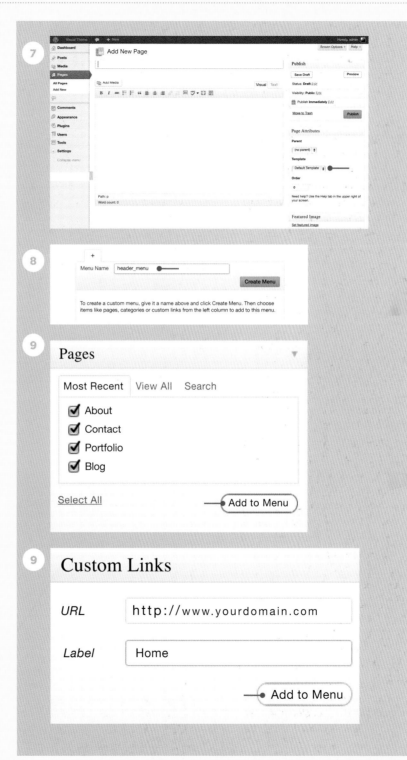

When you are ready, create a second menu entitled "social_menu." You can create custom menu items to include each of the social media platforms you use (e.g. Facebook, Twitter, Google+, etc.) with the "Custom Links" box in the same way you created a home page link; however this time, you type your Facebook page, etc. web address into the URL field rather than your own domain name, and then type "Facebook" in the "Label" field, and so on for all the other social media links you want to include.

Reorder the social media links once you have added them to the "social_menu," and when you've finished, click "Save Menu."

11. You are now ready to create your blog posts and portfolio entries.

First, let's take a look at the layout of the home page so you can see what will go where (see the screenshot at top right).

In the large image space at the top of the page, you will see the featured images of the blog posts or portfolio entries you have chosen for display in the "Slider" (1). An extract from your most recent blog post, plus its featured image if it has one, will go to the right of this (2). Underneath (3), a maximum of six portfolio entries will show up in one or two rows (you can include as many as you like for the portfolio section of the site, but the six most recent blog posts are what will be visible on the home page). Note that you can add explanations and text to the portfolio entries, but the wording will not

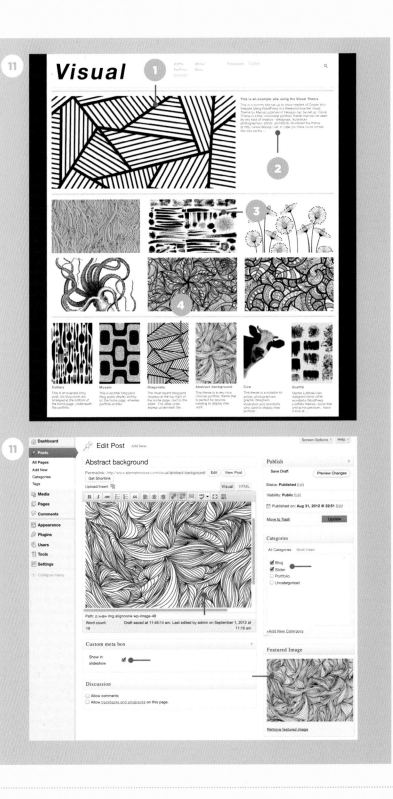

show up on the front page—only on the individual page for that entry.

Finally, across the bottom of the page (4), your six most recent blog posts will appear, along with the first few lines of accompanying text.

In order to define what goes where, you will need to create three post categories. Go to Posts > Categories, and create and save categories entitled "Slider," "Blog," and "Portfolio."

Now, create your entries. For each one, you will need to add a featured image, using the "Featured Image" box bottom right of your screen. You can also add an image, or as many images as you like, plus text, into the main text area of each entry; these will be visible when the visitor visits each entry's individual page.

Using the "Categories" box, assign each entry to one or more of the categories you have just set up. If you are assigning one to the "Slider," you also need to check the box entitled "Show in slideshow" in the "Custom meta box" lower down on the page (as in the screenshot shown).

12. **When** you're satisfied with the look of your portfolio and blog entries, go back and finalize your main pages. You should now activate Jetpack so you can set up a contact form, and also activate Akismet, but once you have done these final touches, you are finished.

With its minimalist layout, the theme does not have space allocated for the addition of widgets; the designer believes they interfere with the cleanness of the whole and detract from your artworks.

Now that you are done, you can enjoy showing off your stunning portfolio site!

Magazine THEME

DEMO: "STRUCTURE" THEME
(free and premium versions, with additional features also available)
by Organic Themes
http://www.organicthemes.com/ theme/structure-theme

A beautiful, responsive, magazine-style theme designed to lay out an enticing array of images, videos, and posts for your site visitors.

You can see the functioning demo of this theme at:

http://www.createyourwebsiteinaweekend. com/structure

PREMIUM VERSION OF "STRUCTURE THEME"

The premium version of this theme offers an image or video slider at the top of the page, which enables you to display more than one featured post, multiple page templates—including a portfolio layout, enhanced layout options, and a choice of black or white versions of the theme— and you also get access to a support forum. (The black version of the theme can be seen on page 98.)

This theme can be translated into any language using the Codestyling Localization plugin—see page 152. (Remember to follow the extra steps applicable only to this theme, as detailed.)

Even the free version of the "Structure" theme looks great on a smartphone or tablet.

"Structure" Theme by Organic Themes (free version).

Our demo site using the "Structural" theme.

HOW TO SET UP AND CUSTOMIZE THE THEME

1. Download the free version of the theme from the Organic Themes site (see the link provided). If you are working on a Mac, your computer will unzip the theme for you; however you need it to be zipped, so zip it again by right-clicking on the "organic_structure _free_v3" folder and choosing "Compress organic_structure_ free_v3."

2. Upload the theme by going to Appearance > Themes > Install Themes > Upload. Click "Choose File," select the "organic_structure_ free_v3.zip" file, then click "Install Now," and then "Activate."

3. When you have uploaded the theme, you will see a link entitled "Customize;" this lets you complete a number of customizations in "Preview" mode without having them be visible on the live site. But let's go straight into the main admin section, as we can do many more customizations from there.

First, you need to install a back-end plugin that will allow you to customize many aspects of the site. Now, click on Appearance > Theme Options. You will see a sentence asking you to install the "Options Framework" plugin—click the red "Install Now" button in the window that pops up, and then click "Activate Plugin."

Go back again to Appearance > Theme Options; you will now see a range of available options. But before we dive into the more complex configuration, we should take care of a few preliminaries.

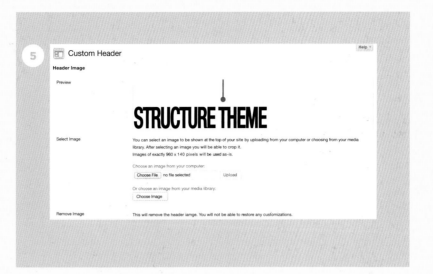

4. As with the demo site, you need to set the date and time, your comments preferences, your permalinks, and so on (see pages 42–45).

5. Next, upload your logo via the Appearance > Header area. Alternatively, you can upload a header panel to go across the entire width of your website; as with the demo site, you can do your cropping within the admin area once you have uploaded your header image. However, it is most likely that you will want to create a header with lettering in it—your name or your site title—in which case you will need to create it separately with another software, such as Pixlr (see page 50), setting the dimensions of your header at 960 x 140 pixels.

If you are uploading a logo, however, I suggest you prepare it beforehand on a transparent background with a height of 140 pixels, with the logo itself at the bottom of the image (see the way the creators of this theme have arranged the "Structure" theme wording—this is to make sure the spacing looks right when you upload the logo).

6. Now, go to Appearance > Background, and either choose the color for the background of your site, or upload a background image (set it to "Tile" so that it covers the entire background area).

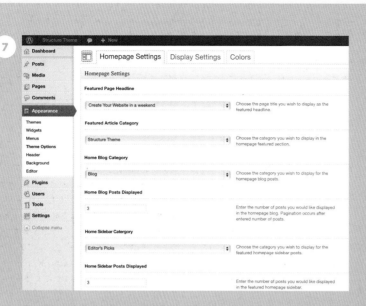

The "Theme Options" area of the "Structure" theme admin.

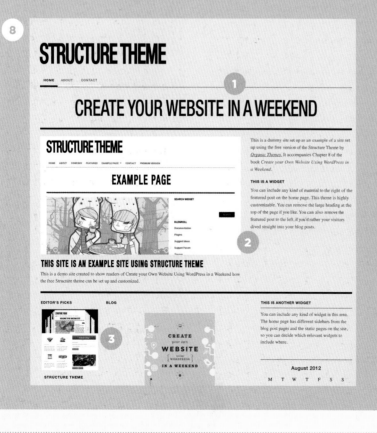

This theme works very well with a background pattern, but note that the background will fill the entire area behind the header, the menu, and the wording, so make sure the color is light, or that it is entirely different from the gray of the menu. It's also crucial that your chosen background doesn't render the writing too difficult to read.

7. Now, for some of the more advanced customization: first, you need to decide if you want to include the large heading on your site (1, left). If you do, you need to create a page (Pages > Add New) using the page title you want to appear on the home page. You will also need to create content for that page to go with the title, as the title will be clickable, meaning that visitors will be able to go to the page.

Once you've created this new page, go to Appearance > Theme Options and select this page from the "Featured Page Headline" drop-down menu. Then click "Save Options" at the bottom of the page.

If you don't want to include the heading on the home page, click on the "Display Settings" tab from within the "Theme Options" area, and uncheck the box labeled 'Display Page Headline?" Then click the "Save Options" button.

8. Next, do you want to include the area towards the top of the page, where you can see a large screenshot on the example site, with text to the right of it (2)? If you do, you first need to create a blog post category (Posts > Categories) specifically for this. Then create a single blog post (Posts > Add New), which you then assign to the new category. You could entitle the new category "Featured," but bear in mind that the category title will show up if you choose to display your post categories as a widget anywhere on the site—therefore, you may wish to give it a more meaningful title.

When you create the post, you will need to add an image to it that will be visible on the main page. If you choose a vertical image, it should be cropped to 620 x 350 pixels to fit the image area. In order to get the image to look right, you can crop the image to fit these dimensions from within the Media Library. Add the image as a "Featured Image" in the box near the bottom-right area of the post-editing page.

Alternatively, you may prefer to add a video to the post that will show up in the image area—if so, just paste your video embed code in the box at the bottom of the editing page instead of adding a featured image. (For YouTube, Share (under the video) > Embed, copy code; for Vimeo, Share/Embed (on the side of the video), copy code.)

Once you have created the post and assigned it to the new category, go back to the "Theme Options" area and select the new category from the "Featured Article Category" drop-down menu, then click the blue button to save. Note that you can only include a single post to display in the featured area.

You can add widgets (Appearance > Widgets) to the area to the right of the featured post.

If you prefer to let your blog posts take primary position on the page instead of including the featured area, go to the "Display Options" tab and uncheck the box labeled "Display Featured Article and Widgets?" Then, click "Save Options."

9. Now you need to create another blog post category for the blog posts to appear in the main area of your website's home page. Go to Posts > Categories, and click "Edit" under the category entitled "Uncategorized" (hover your mouse over the area and the link will appear), then rename the category "Blog," "News," or any other name you prefer, and also rename the "slug." (Be aware that the category name will appear on the home page right above your first blog post, so make sure you choose a meaningful name.) Then, save your changes.

(Note: The advantage of renaming the "Uncategorized" category is that blog posts will automatically get put into that category, unless you assign them to a different or additional category.)

Next, you need to create at least one blog post you can assign to the new category (it can be a dummy post at this stage, which you can work on further later). As before, the main image assigned to the post that will appear in the main area needs to be added via the "Featured Image" box.

Once you have created at least one blog post, go back to the "Theme Options" area and select the new category from the "Home Blog Category" drop-down menu (if a category has no blog posts assigned to it, it will not appear here, which is why you need to create a post before completing this step).

In the field underneath this, you can also choose how many blog posts you want to appear on the home page. When there are more blog posts than the number you've selected, numbers will appear at the bottom of the home page to allow visitors to view previous posts. Click the blue button when you're done.

10. Next, if you want to display a selection of blog posts in the left-hand sidebar (3), first create a new blog category, and then assign at least one new blog post to it, as before. The title of the new category will appear above the entries in the left-hand sidebar (again, it should be a title that makes sense to your viewers).

You can, of course, assign existing blog posts that already belong to the previous category to the new category, but this will cause some repetition on the home page, as the same posts will appear in the main area as to the side.

Once you have created the blog posts for the sidebar, select the new category from the "Home Sidebar Category" drop-down menu in the "Theme Options" area. As before, in the field underneath this, you can choose how many blog posts you want to include here. Save as usual when you're done.

If you do not want to include any blog posts in the left-hand sidebar, you can uncheck the "Display Sidebar Posts?" box under the "Display Options" tab. (You can put widgets in the sidebar as well as, or instead of, blog posts.)

11. **There** are a few more settings inside "Display Settings," and these concern social media. If you look at your site, you will notice that the theme automatically includes buttons that allow visitors to recommend your site on Facebook, Twitter, or Google+. If you do not want these to appear on your home page, your static pages, or your blog posts, you can configure this here—it is your choice whether you wish to include them. Click the blue "Save Options" button if you decide to deactivate any.

12. **Finally**, the last tab in the "Theme Options" area allows you to make some color changes to the different kinds of links on your site; if you make any changes, click the button, as usual, to save them.

13. **Now**, you need to set up your menu (Appearance > Menus). As with the demo site, first create a menu, which you can name whatever you like, and then save it. (There is no need to assign the menu to a certain position on the page, as we did with the demo site, so you can just ignore the "Theme Locations" box on the menu page.)

You will probably want to create some static pages for your site (e.g. "About" and "Contact"); now is the time to do this so you can add them to the menu—you can always adjust their content later.

When you have created static pages for your site, add them to the menu from within the "Pages" box. (You will probably not want to include the page that you created specifically to give the large title on the home page, but if you do want to add it to the menu, you can do so.)

To create a "Home" link for the menu, first create a "Custom" link inside the "Custom Links" box, using your domain as the URL and the title "Home" as the label (see the screenshot to the left). Click "Add to Menu," then reorder the items in menu, and save. (With this theme, you need to create a custom link for the menu, because there is no "Home" page as such; this is because the theme automatically puts certain elements together from other areas of your site to create the home page.)

Note that with this theme, you do not need to create a "Blog" page and assign it to contain the blog posts inside the Settings > Reading area as we did for the demo site with the default theme. This is because the "Structure Theme" automatically displays blog posts on the front page—you don't actually have any other option.

14. Go to Appearance > Widgets. You can see that with this theme, you have many different options as to where you can display your widgets. You can display them on the home page, in the footer area, and on the right-hand side of your static pages. (The Left Sidebar widgets will not show up on your static pages, but they will show up if, for example, your readers click on a category or a tag link, if you choose to display these somewhere on your site).

While you are setting up your widgets, you will probably want to activate the Jetpack plugin suite, as explained when setting up the demo site, so that you can make use of its handy features, such as an easy-to-configure contact form for your contact page, and multiple widget options.

15. Finally, set up Akismet to stop yourself from getting a torrent of comment spam—and you're done!

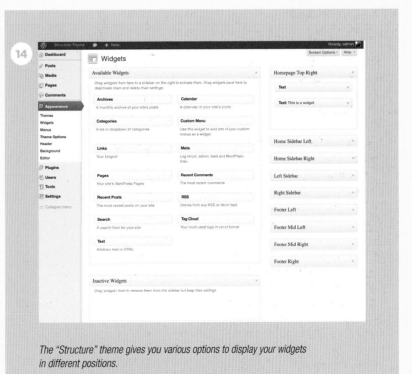

The "Structure" theme gives you various options to display your widgets in different positions.

e-commerce THEME

DEMO: "MYSTILE" THEME
(free) by WooThemes
http://www.woothemes.com/products/mystile

"Mystile" is an elegant and professional e-commerce theme designed to work hand in hand with the WooCommerce plugin. The theme offers a high level of customization and will suit any kind of web store.

You can view the functioning demo of this theme at: http://www.createyourwebsiteinaweekend.com/mystile

This theme can be translated into any language using the Codestyling Localization plugin—see page 152.

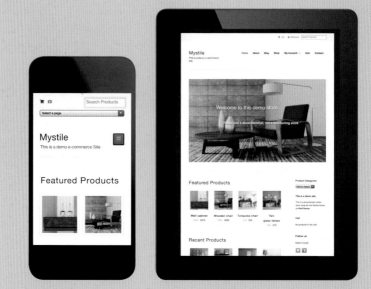

"Mystile" is a responsive theme so your site will look gorgeous on a smartphone or a tablet, as shown.

"Mystile" theme by WooThemes.

Our demo site using the "Mystile" theme.

HOW TO SET UP AND CUSTOMIZE THE THEME

1. Download the theme from the WooThemes website (see the link provided). If you are working on a Mac, your computer will unzip the theme for you; however, you need it to be zipped, so zip it again by right-clicking on the "Mystile" folder and choosing "Compress Mystile."

2. Upload the theme by going to Appearance > Themes > Install Themes > Upload. Click "Choose File," select the zip file, then click "Install Now," and then "Activate."

3. You will see a screen full of different customization options, but before we look at these, notice an invitation at the top of the screen asking you to download the free WooDojo plugin—click the "Get WooDojo" button. (If you can't see the invitation, go to http://www.woothemes.com/woodojo.) WooDojo is a suite of tools produced by the WooThemes team; while we can install the WooCommerce plugin independently of WooDojo, it makes sense to install the WooDojo suite in its entirety, so that you have the option of using its other features also.

4. Download the plugin and install it (Plugins > Add new > Upload > Choose File > Install Now > Activate Plugin). (If you are working on a Mac, just as with a theme, your computer will unzip the plugin folder for you, but as you need it zipped, right-click and compress it to zip it up again.)

5. Click on the new WooDojo link now visible in your left-hand navigation.

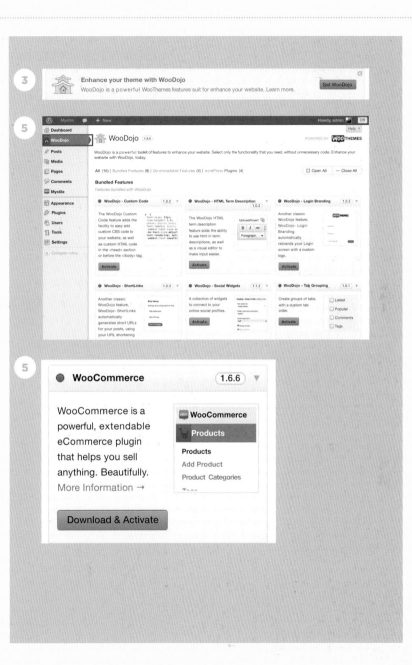

Scroll down to the bottom of the page, where you will see a box entitled "WooCommerce"—click the blue "Download & Activate" button (as seen in the screenshot).

6. Click the purple button entitled "Install WooCommerce Pages."

7. You now have everything in place for your online store. Now let's customize the look of your site before we set up the e-commerce part and start adding products. Click on Mystile > Theme Options.

8. To customize the theme, follow these steps:

i. First, go to General Settings > Quick Start. Here you can adjust the color with the "Theme Stylesheet" drop-down; the default color for the menu links and touches throughout the site is orange, which I have changed to gray for the demo site. You can also upload a logo here or choose to stick with the written title; the image you upload will shrink to fit the allocated space.

Note: we will talk about tracking your site visitors later in the book. You can come back and insert your Google Analytics tracking code here.

On the "Display Options" screen, you can choose whether to enable a breadcrumb trail on the site. Breadcrumbs are a navigation aid that show your visitor where they are in a site, however it only makes sense to show them if your site is large and you have many product subcategories.

On this screen, you can also choose whether to display comments on your posts and pages, and whether to show just blog excerpts or the entire entry on your blog page. You don't need to do anything in the "Custom CSS" field; this is

Customizing the "Mystile" theme.

mainly for web developers making changes to colors and other items on the site using code.

ii. Under Styling Options > Background, you can choose a background color or image. Set your background image to repeat, and then choose whether it should move or should remain fixed when the site visitor scrolls down the page. Note that the background color or image you choose for the site won't show up until you check "Enable Boxed Layout" under the "Layout Options" tab.

Under Styling Options > Links, you can choose to change your link and button colors. "Link Hover Color" is the color a link changes to when the user moves their mouse over a link. It will be easier to change your button color when you have the site set up with some products and you can see how your live site looks, so you may want to come back to this later.

iii. Under the "Typography" tab, you can change the fonts displayed on the site. For the demo site, for example, I changed the font from Arial to Helvetica throughout, and I also reduced the blog post titles.

iv. Under "Layout Options," you can add a frame to your site, which will make the background color or image visible—you can also choose whether to have the sidebar on the left- or the right-hand side on pages where you have chosen to include a sidebar.

For the "Category Exclude" fields, you will want to add "Uncategorized" to your list of categories that should not show up on your home page or blog, as this looks clumsy and unprofessional.

v. Now go to Homepage > Featured image. You can choose whether to have a large image visible at the top of the home page, as on the demo site—if so, check the box labeled "Display a banner on the home page?" then upload your image and decide what wording (if any) you want to add to run across it. Ideally, the image should not be too high, as a very large image will take up a disproportionate amount of space on your home page.

Note: when choosing or taking a photograph for this space, bear in mind that you will have to crop it into a horizontal rectangle.

The "Sidebar," "Products," and "Blog" tabs allow you to decide what content you will display on your home page. You can come back to this later once you have added some products to your store and have some fun playing around with the different options.

Here, I have included two blog entries on the front page of the demo site; including blog posts on your home page may not be suitable for all types of e-commerce sites, but it can be a good way to add some personal interest to the front page of an online store, which can otherwise look a bit dry—it will help this page look more dynamic.

vi. Under the "WooCommerce" tab, you will have the same "Products" screen as appears under the "Home" tab, but there is also another screen that allows you to choose whether or not to have sidebars appearing on your "Products" and "Archive" pages.

vii. You do not need to change anything on the "Dynamic Images" tab.

viii. "Footer Customization" allows you to decide how many columns you'd like to display in the footer area. You can also choose to replace the default left and right text at the bottom of the page with your own text. Since this is a free theme, I have decided to leave the "WooThemes" credit; however I did choose to include an affiliate link in the "Custom Affiliate Link" field (you can sign up as an affiliate on the WooThemes site, meaning that if anyone makes a purchase following clicking on the link on your website, you will get a cut of the sale).

ix. In the "Subscribe & Connect" area, you can set up the social media links to put in your sidebar as a widget; you can also ask your visitors to subscribe to your MailChimp newsletter (see Chapter 9).

x. I suggest you skip the "Advertising" tab, because it makes no sense to include Google or any other ads on your own online store. (Why would you want to drive potential customers away from purchasing your products?) But if you did wish to run ads on your site, here is where you would put the code.

xi. Finally, under the "Contact" tab, you can put your email address for the built-in contact form on the contact page you will set up shortly.

xii. In the main navigation, under the "Mystile" tab, there is an "SEO" menu item; you will understand how to configure this once you have read the "Search Engine Optimization" pages in the next chapter. Alternatively, you can use the All in One SEO Pack plugin that we will look at in detail; if you prefer to use this, you will need to check the box labeled "Use 3rd Party Plugin Data."

xiii. The last thing you will want to look at inside the Mystile configuration area is the "Sidebars Manager." "Mystile" allows you to create different sidebars, to which you will then be able to add widgets (inside the Appearance > Widgets area). Here, I have not set up custom sidebars on the demo; however, you may find them useful—for example, to show different widgets to the side of your blog pages than those you will show on your "Products" pages.

You do not need to make any changes to any of the other areas within the Mystile configuration area.

9. Now that you've customized many aspects of the look of your site, it's time to set up WooCommerce. Go to WooCommerce > Settings.

WooCommerce is a full-featured plugin that allows you a wealth of options for the management of your online store, such as inventory control, order management, and many more. You will want to explore your options in detail; if you have any queries, you may want to refer to the documentation (see the web address below the screenshot bottom right).

To get set up, you need to set the following options:

i. Under the "General" tab, set your country and currency, and choose the countries from which you will accept orders.

ii. Under the "Catalog Options" tab, set your country-specific elements such as currency sign position, and the thousand and decimal separators used for your currency.

iii. Under "Tax," choose whether you want your prices to include taxes, or to list them separately, and then set up the relevant taxes.

iv. Under "Shipping," select the shipping or delivery methods you will allow and what you will charge for them.

v. Under "Payment Gateways," set your PayPal email and specify whether you will allow other payment methods such as by transfer, check, or cash on delivery. When you start taking orders, you will find them listed in the "Orders" area. Your sales reports, customers, and stock inventory are all recorded under "Reports."

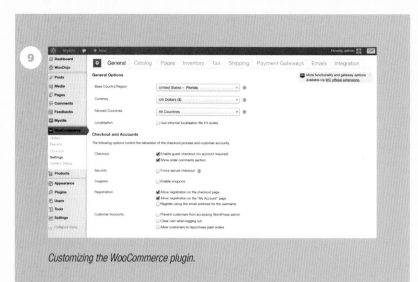

Customizing the WooCommerce plugin.

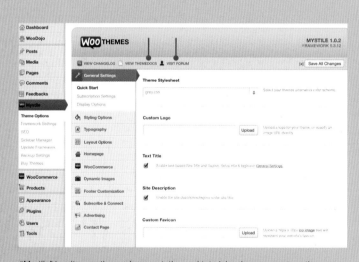

"Mystile" has its own theme documentation and tutorials, plus a support section, accessed by clicking the "View Themedocs" or "Visit Forum" links. WooCommerce has its own documentation and support forum at http://wcdocs.woothemes.com.

10. With your basic settings in order, you are ready to add products to your store. Before you do this, go to the "Settings" area and set your permalinks to "Post name" so that your website URLs will have meaningful names like "http://www.yourdomain/shop/turquoise-chair," rather than a string of dates or numbers. While you are in the "Settings" area, make sure your title, date,

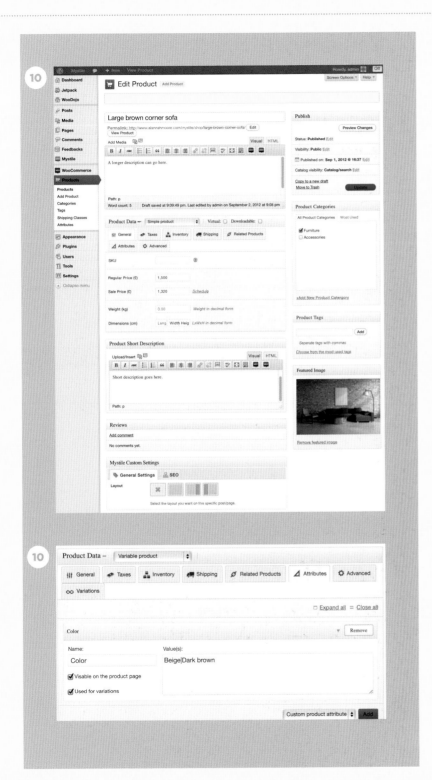

time, name/comments/search engines preferences are as they should be (as we did on pages 42–45 for the demo site).

Next, set your product categories (Products > Categories); you can add an image for each category, then create the products (Products > Add Product), assigning them to the correct categories. When adding a product, use the "Featured Image" box for the main image (on the right-hand side of the screenshot). You can add a description of the product in the regular editing box, a short description in the "Product Short Description" box, the price in the "Product Data" area, as well as additional photos or even a photo gallery (in the same way as you would add an image gallery to a blog post—see page 64).

It's useful to know how to set a product variation (for example, different colors or sizes). First, select "Variable Product" from the drop-down next to "Product Data," as shown in the screenshot below left. Then click the "Attributes" tab. Click the blue "Add" button, then name the attribute (as in the example, where I am adding the color options of the sofa to be ordered), then add the values, separated by a "|" (I have specified the options of beige or dark brown). Check the checkboxes next to "Visible on the product page" and "Used for variations" and click the "Save attributes" button. Then click the "Variations" tab, choose your default, and click "Add Variation." Now add the price and any other details, and click the "Publish" or "Update" button to save the product.

	Image	Name	SKU	Stock	Price	Categories	Tags	★	🛒	Date
☐		**Brown sofa** ID: 47 | Quick Edit | Trash | View | Duplicate		In stock	From ~~1,400~~ ~~1,300~~	Furniture		☆		2012/09/01 Published
☐		Green sofa		In stock	~~£1,200~~ £1,150	Furniture		☆		2012/09/01 Published
☐		Large brown corner sofa		In stock	~~£1,500~~ £1,320	Furniture		☆		2012/09/01 Published
☐		Two-seater white leather sofa		In stock	~~£1,400~~ £1,300	Furniture		━● ☆		2012/09/01 Published
☐		Wall cabinet		In stock	£300 £275	Furniture		━● ★		2012/09/01 Published

You can select a product as "Featured" by clicking the star that appears next to it in the "Products" view (as shown on the screenshot). As you would with a blog post, you can also make quick edits by hovering over the space underneath the product title with your mouse, and clicking the "Quick Edit" link.

11. After you've added your products, the next step is to set up your pages and then make them visible on the site by attaching them either to the main menu or to a small menu at the top of the site.

First, let's look at your pages. Go to Pages > All Pages; you will see that WooCommerce has automatically created a number of pages for you that relate to the functioning of the store. You may not want to include absolutely all of these in your store; we'll see about that in a moment.

Now, create the other pages needed for your site (e.g. "About," "Blog," "Contact," "Privacy," and "Terms & Conditions"). When you create your "Blog" page, don't forget to assign it the blog layout, which you do in the "Page Attributes" box at the same time you create the page (it's down at the lower right on the editing page). The same goes for the "Contact" page—this has a layout incorporating a form created especially for it, which you select in the same way from the "Page Attributes" box.

Note: it will reduce the likelihood of canceled orders if you can add a telephone number to your "Contact" page, as well as a visible email address, as we did with the demo site, using the Email Protector plugin.

Once you have created these pages, you can assign them to the correct menus so that they show up on the site. Go to the Appearance > Menus area and create two menus, which

you can title "Primary" and "Top." Assign these to the correct locations in the "Theme Locations" box to the left. The smaller menu that runs along the top of the page will be ideal for "Terms & Conditions" links, whereas the main pages of the site, together with the store links, will go into the main menu.

Scroll down the page a little to look at the "Pages" box on the left. Here you will see the pages you have just created, together with the store pages WooCommerce created for you. You may not want all of these to appear in the menu—the choice is yours. As we did with the demo site, check the pages you want to include and then add them to the menu by clicking the button. In the screenshot (facing page), you can see how I chose to arrange the pages on the main menu in the demo store, which may help you as a guideline; you may wish to include different store pages, or to arrange them differently.

In addition to these elements, if you have a large number of categories of products, you may want to create custom menu links and add them as drop-down items underneath your "Shop" menu so your visitors can easily find the category of product they are looking for. When you're done, save your menus and move on to the next step.

12. **The final** addition to your site will be to set up your sidebars and widgets. The theme gives you one standard sidebar, but you can create different sidebars, that will appear on different pages, by adding the WooSidebars plugin via the WooDojo area. (After installing and activating the plugin, go to Appearance > Widget Areas and create your new sidebars from here.) Then go to the "Widgets" area, where you will see that the theme comes with a selection of widgets of its own—here you can choose to add a shopping cart, bestsellers, recently viewed products, and other e-commerce widgets into the sidebars or footer. You may choose to activate some of the WooDojo elements, such as the "Tab" widget, or their "Social" widget; and you will probably also want to activate Jetpack so that you can use some of its widgets.

13. **You** will want to create some blog posts so that there is some content in the blog area.

14. **Don't** forget to set up Akismet, as we did with the demo site in Chapter 5, so that you don't drown in comment spam.

15. **Finally,** when everything else is in place, run a test order to

You may wish to arrange your pages something like this; you will also need to create a "Custom" link to your home page (http://yourdomain.com).

check that everything is working properly, and also so that you'll be familiar with the ordering process and will know what will happen when you get your first customer. There are two easy ways to do this: either set up a product with a very low price and actually go through the purchase steps yourself (PayPal has a "sandbox" specifically for testing, but setting up a single dummy order is much quicker and easier to do). Alternatively, you can enable payment by check and make an order as if you were a customer choosing to manually mail in a check. If everything is working as it should be, you are ready to go!

MANAGING YOUR STORE
You will manage orders coming from your working store from inside the WooCommerce > Orders area. Here, you can keep track of your orders by marking the status of each—Pending, On-hold, Processing, Completed, etc.—as well as adding notes, as needed. Sales details (over specified time periods, as well as details of top selling and top earning products) and customer statistics can be seen in the Reports area, as well as inventory reports under the "Stock" tab; discount coupons are created in the Coupons area.

9

Your live site

SPREADING THE WORD AND ATTRACTING VISITORS

Growing your AUDIENCE

Bravo! You now have your shiny new website up and running, ready for your first visitors. But how do you get people to come to your website? And how do you keep them coming back?

Imagine you're opening a brick-and-mortar store. Unless you're on a deserted road out in the sticks or completely hidden away up a tiny alleyway somewhere, you can always rely on at least a small amount of passing trade. Once you open your doors, someone, at some point, will come in to see who you are and what you are doing.

Unfortunately, this is not at all true for a website: you can spend days making it as gorgeous and interesting as you want, but unless you let people know, not one single person, ever, will find out about it and visit you.

You could say that marketing is the lifeblood of a real-world business, but it's even more true of a website. Without marketing, your website stands no chance.

So, how *do* you get people to come to your site?

ONLINE MARKETING TECHNIQUES

Here are some ways you can use the internet to drive visitors to your new website:

1. Make your website search-engine-friendly.

The most obvious way for people to come across your website is via the search engines. Your site needs to appear in search engines, as high up in the listing as you can manage, and for the key words and phrases people will be using when they are looking for a website or service like yours. See page 137 for details on how you can optimize your site for the search engines (a practice known as "SEO").

2. Publicize your website using social media services.

Facebook, Twitter, Google+, LinkedIn, and other social media are phenomenally useful publicity tools. We'll see more about using these on page 143.

3. Advertising.

You can advertise your site online using a service such as Google AdWords. These are the adverts you see at the top and on the right-hand side of Google when you conduct a search; you pay per click, which is each time a person clicks on the advert to visit your site, hence this type of advertising is known as "Pay Per Click," or "PPC." This can be a very effective way of getting traffic to your site, and you can specify your budget to make sure you don't overspend too.

Google is by far the most important search engine—85 percent of all web searches are conducted via Google.

The entries on the top and right-hand sides of your Google search results are paid-for ads (Google AdWords).

Google AdWords is a good way to get traffic to your site immediately; you can specify a daily budget to keep control of your costs.

Google and the Google logo are registered trademarks of Google Inc., used with permission.

4. Get yourself listed or mentioned on other people's websites.

A great way to get new visitors to your site is to get your products or services talked about on someone else's website, preferably in the form of a recommendation or favorable review. How you will approach the owner of the site obviously depends on what your business is and the kind of site you have created, as well as whether you have had prior contact; a personal introduction via email will probably be the way to begin.

The Technorati Blog Directory lists blogs in all fields of interest.

You will also want to get your site listed in portal-type websites and (again, depending on if this is appropriate for you) exchange links with other sites in your field of interest. (Obviously, you don't want to send your website visitors to your direct competitors, but there are usually other complementary businesses you could usefully exchange website links with.)

5. Leave comments on other people's blogs and participate in forums.

Although this will depend on the kind of site you have created, leaving constructive comments at the bottom of posts on other people's blogs and participating in online forum discussions can help introduce new potential site visitors to you as a reliable and useful source of information on your specialist subject matter. Internet etiquette demands that you never blatantly promote your site, your services, or your products, but leave genuinely useful information—followed, of course, by a discreet "signature" containing a link to your website.

6. Write guest posts for other people's blogs.

Writing a "guest post" for someone else's blog can be an amazingly successful way of bringing yourself to the attention of a large audience in the same field of interest as you. To have your offer accepted, you will have to prove that what you write will be of special interest, but if you're successful, you may be able to attract a large number of interested and curious people to your site or your own blog.

7. Give away freebies.

Whether it's an e-book, free advice, or a free consultation, giving away something for free is a good way to publicize your site. If what you are offering has genuine value, there is a chance it could "go viral" (circulate quickly from person to person), which will then bring dozens of new visitors to your site.

8. Include an email signature.

This sounds pretty basic, but it's surprising how many people neglect to do this. Set your email software so that at the bottom of every single email you send out, your website address appears as a "signature"—people can easily visit it by clicking on the link.

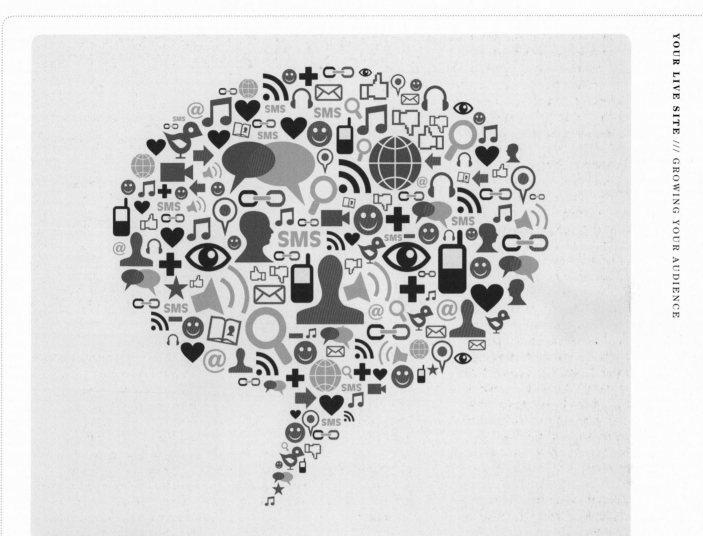

OFFLINE MARKETING

Don't overlook old-fashioned ways of marketing your website. In fact, you will need to exploit these from the off to kick-start a stream of traffic to your site.

1. **Mention** your website to everyone you know, and to every new person you meet.
2. **Carry** postcards or business cards with your web address on it, and give them out whenever possible.
3. **Distribute** brochures or fliers in appropriate places.
4. **Don't be shy**—ask people you know to tell their friends about you, or to help distribute your postcards or business cards to their friends. Personal recommendation can be a powerful tool.
5. **Find** a newsworthy aspect of what you are doing, and send out press releases to your local newspaper.
6. **Create a wonderful**, informative site, and if you are selling from your site, give your customers the best products and the best customer service they could wish for. That way, your reputation will grow by itself, simply by word of mouth.

Maintaining relationships with your VISITORS

It's great to get website visitors, but what you really want is to create a loyal band of visitors who come back to your site repeatedly. Out of the hundreds of sites people will visit, how do you guarantee they'll remember yours and come back? Here are some ideas.

1. Start an email newsletter.

One way to get people to remember you is to keep in touch by email. To do this, you'll need to capture their email address from your website, which means you will need an external mailing-list manager to manage the list of addresses you'll acquire.

There are a number of email-list managers out there; AWeber and MailChimp are the major players. MailChimp is great for starting out as it is free until you get 2,000 subscribers, providing you don't send out more than 12,000 emails a month. (It also has a selection of delightfully juicy-looking templates you can use for your newsletters.) However, AWeber has the more sophisticated tracking tools of the two, which you might find suits your needs better—especially if you can see your list growing large quickly, at which point the price difference becomes negligible.

AWeber and MailChimp are the major players in the email-marketing arena.

EMAIL MARKETING SERVICE PROVIDERS

Here are a few well-known email marketing services; the one you choose will depend on your needs and your budget:

AWeber *http://www.aweber.com*
MailChimp *http://mailchimp.com*
Constant Contact *http://www.constantcontact.com*
iContact *https://www.icontact.com*
Campaign Monitor *http://www.campaignmonitor.com*
Benchmark *http://www.benchmarkemail.com*
Pinpointe *http://www.pinpointe.com*
GetResponse *http://www.getresponse.com*
Vertical Response *http://www.verticalresponse.com*

PLAY BY THE RULES

When sending out your newsletter you need to observe email etiquette and stick to the rules.

> It's important not to sign anyone up to your email list without their agreement.

> Never trick your readers with misleading subject lines.

> Your email should display a real address.

> Let them know how they can "opt out" of your list—and act on "unsubscribe" requests promptly.

> You need to make sure you adhere to the rules laid down by the CAN-SPAM Act—see page 146 for more information.

Don't just email people from your regular email account—you'll find it incredibly difficult to keep track of subscribe and unsubscribe requests once you get any number of subscribers. You will also find it really hard to prove people actually gave you permission to add their email address to your list if you are challenged at any point. You really don't want to be accused of spamming.

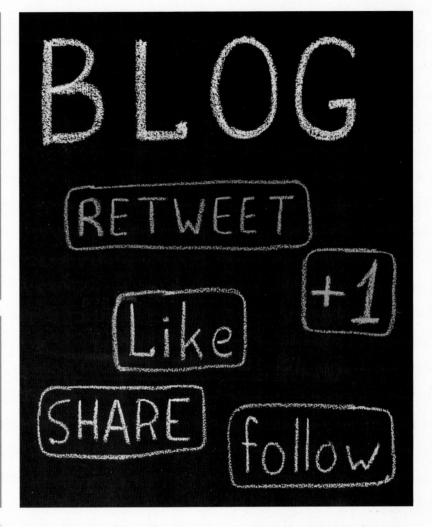

TIP

Both AWeber and MailChimp have plugins that allow you to integrate your sign-up form into your WordPress site (AWeber Web Form Plugin, MailChimp List Subscribe Form). Both allow you to deliver your blog posts automatically to your readers by email, as well as send out newsletters as often as you like.

2. Start a blog on your site.

We have talked about blogs throughout this book, but there will be a number of readers who feel that a blog is not for them. As I see it, there is no better way to engage your readers than with an up-to-date blog; even the most serious of business sites will find there is sector-specific information valuable to their visitors that they can post in a "news" area. See the box on the next page.

3. Invite your visitors to subscribe to your blog.

Visitors can subscribe to your blog and read your posts using an RSS feed reader (see glossary), but for most people, it will be much easier for them to receive your blog posts by email.

The easiest way to put a sign-up form on your blog is via the Jetpack "Subscriptions" widget. (Of course, this won't apply if you're going to

THE BENEFITS OF INCLUDING A BLOG ON YOUR WEBSITE

> Google loves blog content. It provides more relevant, keyword-rich material for your site, and it's constantly changing.
> Your visitors or clients will like to see that you're up to date with developments in your area.
> It presents you as authority in your area.
> Your readers can comment and interact with you. A blog is much more engaging and personal than the static part of your website.
> Cataloging what you're working on gives you a chance to demonstrate your achievements.
> It also gives you the opportunity to do useful market research by asking your potential clients what they need or want.
> If your posts are frequent and interesting, you'll attract regular readers. As well as increasing your traffic, this gives you more of a chance to engage your readers as clients, or do business with them again.

SUBSCRIBE TO BLOG VIA EMAIL

Enter your email address to subscribe to this blog and recieve notifications of new posts by email.

Subscribe

The Jetpack "Subscriptions" widget

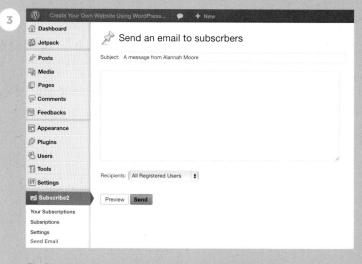

The Subscribe2 plugin lets you email your subscribers directly.

integrate your blog subscribers with your email list.)

Alternatively, you can install the Subscribe2 plugin; enable the widget on the Subscribe2 > Settings page to add it to your sidebars.

This plugin offers you more options than the simple Jetpack version: you can customize the emails your subscribers will receive, access their email addresses, and email them with announcements outside the blog (though don't abuse this—strictly speaking, your subscribers have signed up for blog posts rather than updates from you.).

4. Make use of social media.
Social media is one of the best ways of keeping your visitors engaged. Once someone has "liked" you on Facebook or followed you on Twitter, you have a means of notifying them whenever you have anything newsworthy to pass on. We'll go into details about social media on page 142.

5. Give your visitors a reason to come back.
Start a regular feature, such as a weekly or monthly roundup of useful tools or book picks, for example, or an analysis of news in your domain. Alternatively, you could run a competition and announce the results on your site on a specified date.

Tracking your VISITORS

As your site traffic grows, you'll want to see where your visitors are coming from. The easiest way to do this is via the WordPress.com "Stats" plugin that comes with Jetpack. It provides you with basic information: how many visitors you've had each day; if they've been referred from another website that links to you; if they came as a result of a search engine; which key word it was that led them to your website; and which pages and posts on your site are the most popular.

If you want more detailed information, such as where your site visitors are located and what time of day they visited, Google Analytics is what you need—it'll provide you with as many statistics as you could possibly want.

The Jetpack "Stats" plugin.

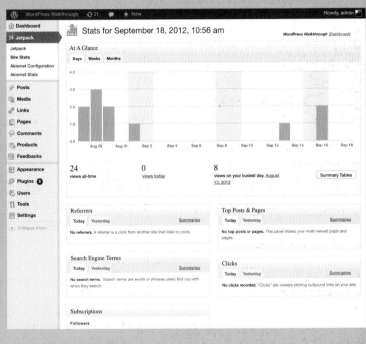

The Jetpack "Stats" screen.

Setting up Google Analytics

1. Sign up for a Google Analytics account here: http://www.google.com/analytics

You have to have a Google account before you can sign up for Google Analytics—you can sign up for this at the same time if you don't already have one.

2. Create an account for your website, providing the required details; click "Create Account."

3. Copy your tracking ID—the string of letters and numbers beginning with "UA-" (as indicated).

4. Now go to the Plugins > Add New area, and search for the "Google Analytics for WordPress" plugin. Install it and activate it.

5. Either allow or disallow tracking in order to improve the plugin—up to you.

6. Check the small box where it says, "Manually enter your UA code," and then paste in your tracking ID. Click the blue button labeled "Update Google Analytics Settings." You'll now be able to see details about your site visitors at the Google Analytics website (obviously, at this stage it will still say "zero" until it starts to register visitors).

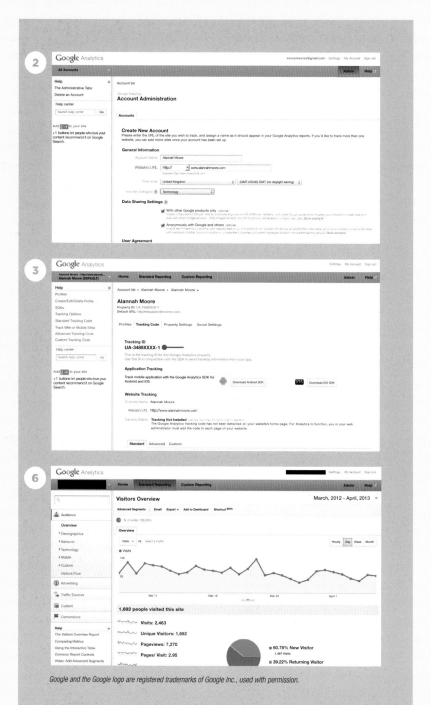

Google and the Google logo are registered trademarks of Google Inc., used with permission.

Search engine optimization (SEO)

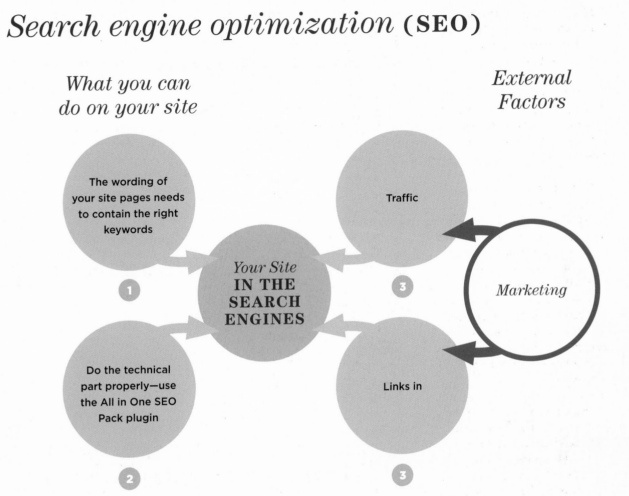

What you can do on your site

1. The wording of your site pages needs to contain the right keywords

2. Do the technical part properly—use the All in One SEO Pack plugin

Your Site IN THE SEARCH ENGINES

External Factors

Traffic — 3

Links in — 3

Marketing

Search Engine Optimization (or "SEO," as it is most commonly known) is, in a nutshell, what you can do to make sure your site gets the best possible position in the search engines. SEO has evolved into a vast and complex science all of its own; I won't be able to cover all the ins and outs here, but I will tell you the basics of what you need to know, and show you how you can prepare your site to best advantage.

This section is divided into three parts. Firstly, you need to identify the key words and phrases for which you will concentrate on getting a good ranking for your website. These need to be incorporated into the actual text that appears on your web pages.

Secondly, there are a number of technical points you need to pay attention to, concerning these key words and phrases and the way you describe your website pages for the search engines. Luckily, a plugin will help you make sure you have these set up the way

they need to be—I'll explain how to configure this. These two areas concern what you can actually do on your website to prepare it for the search engines.

The third area deals with the external factors that will impact your site's ranking in the search engines. You may have less control over these external factors, but the way you market your website will have a serious impact.

Note: there aren't any secret tricks a webmaster can do to ensure a good position, and you can't buy a good site ranking—the best you can do for your site is to make it as interesting and engaging as possible, fill it full of relevant and useful content, and follow the advice in 1–3 below.

1. OPTIMIZING YOUR PAGES WITH YOUR KEY WORDS AND PHRASES

The actual text that is on your website pages is one of the major things the search engines look at when they are trying to classify your website. You therefore need to make sure your pages contain the words and phrases people will most logically use to type into Google, or another search engine, if they are looking for a website such as yours. These are referred to as keywords or key phrases.

To work out what keywords you should focus on for your site, do some brainstorming with a pen and paper to come up with a list of the words and phrases you yourself might use if you were searching for a site like yours. But there's a catch. You can't be too generic, as the internet is a crowded place. If you show up on page ten of Google, people won't find you, so you need to choose keywords that are neither too much in demand, nor so obscure that only a tiny number of people will be looking for them—that way, you might find yourself at the top of the list, but attract only a handful of site visitors.

Let's take an example: if you type "B and B France" into Google, there are 1,360,000,000 results. I would

consider this to be an impossible number of websites to compete with, and that you would stand very little chance of coming up high enough in the listing to get any site visitors at all. However, if we try to be a bit more specific by typing "B and B Normandy," we can see that the number of competitors gets much more reasonable—at 2,950,000, though, this is still pretty challenging.

"B and B Normandy Coast" has a smaller number of sites listed for it—1,440,000—and if we are just a little more specific, we'll find that "B and B Etretat" has even fewer —308,000 sites are returned. So in this case, I consider that concentrating on both "B and B Normandy Coast" and "B and B Etretat" would be a good strategy. We would hope to catch people looking more generally for somewhere to stay along the Normandy coast, as well as people who already know precisely where they want to stay.

You could also get a little bit creative and think of other ways to catch potential visitors—for example, if you Google "Weekend break in Normandy," you will find 260,000 sites listed, so it may be worthwhile including this key phrase as well.

When you have worked out your keywords, take a look at your page text and see how you can rework it. Your major keywords need to be at the top of your home page, preferably in a title, and repeated in the body of the text a couple more times too if possible without it reading strangely. Focus on your major keywords for

your home page; you can choose less-important keywords for the secondary pages on your site—for example, to continue with the previous example, the site owner might create a page listing activities in and around their area, and choose the following key phrases to focus on: "Activities on the Normandy Coast" and "Things to do around Etretat." These pages may attract visitors, and they'll also boost the position of the site as search engines will comprehend the pages as worthwhile and relevant material in the same broad area of interest.

Don't "stuff" your page text full of keywords in a way that makes your text read bizarrely—there is nothing that will annoy or alienate your site visitors more than this.

Google | b and b france | 🔍

Search   About 1,000,000,000 results (0.31 seconds) ●——

"B and B France" has far too many entries to compete with…

Google | b and b normandy coast | 🔍

Search   About 1,440,000,results (0.36 seconds) ●——

…Whereas "B and B Normany Coast" has a little less competition.

Google | b and b normand|y france | 🔍

> b and b normandy france
> b and b normandy
> b and b normandy beaches
> b and b normandia

Search

Web
Images
Videos
News
Shopping

Ads related to **b and b normandy france** ⓘ

750 Hotels in Normandy -Lowest price guarantee
www.booking.com/Normandie-Hotels - ★★★★★ 1,018 seller reviews
Book your Hotel in Normandy online
762 552 people + 1'd or follow Booking.com

Most Popular Hotels   Best Reviewed Hotels
Budget Hotels   Luxury Hotels

Ads ⓘ

Beat Normandy B&Bs
www.housetrip.com/Normand
Beautiful B&B Alternatives! Pl
& Reviews. Book Now From 3
106 people + 1'd or follow
HouseTrip.com

Google gives you some suggestions for keywords and phrases as you type in your search item—it's worth checking these out.

Be realistic in your choice of key words
and phrases to focus on. It's far better
to come up on the first page of Google
for a rather less sought-after key word,
than on page ten for a really obvious one.

2. PAGE TITLES, DESCRIPTIONS, AND KEYWORDS

Now that you have your page text "optimized," it's time to look at the more technical side of things.

We've seen how the text you put into your pages is essential for the search engines; the following technical aspects are also crucial:

> the way you "title" your pages (this is the page title seen at the top of your browser window when you're on a page)
> the "description" you assign to each of your pages (this is the description of each page that you will see listed in Google underneath the page title)
> the key words you choose to associate with the pages (the latter is the least important aspect of the three)

WordPress has a number of plugins that allow you to input this information—the one we will look at here is called "All in One SEO Pack."

Setting up "All in One SEO Pack"

1. **Install** the "All in One SEO Pack" plugin as usual from the Plugins > Add New screen.
2. **Go to** Settings > All in One SEO. Scroll down underneath the adverts and click the "Plugin Status: Enabled" button (see opposite).
3. **Fill** in the "Home Title" field—this is the title that appears at the top of the browser window, which will also be the title of the site as it appears in the search engines. Type your title and ensure it includes your major search terms; don't go over 65 characters,

however, as this is all that will show up.

4. **"Home Description"**—type a slightly longer description of your site, including your keywords in a natural way. This description will show up in some, but not all, of the search engines (it *will* appear in Google, so you should be sure to make it sound enticing). Don't exceed 165 characters.
5. **"Home Keywords"**—put your keywords and phrases here, separated by commas; 20 is the maximum number. Be aware when choosing that unless a key word is actually included in the page text as well, it may not carry any weight.
6. **Skip** to the fields entitled "Post Title Format," "Page Format," and so on. I suggest you remove the "| %blog_title%" part from "%post_title% | %blog_title%," wherever it appears, as this will allow your post and page titles to be more targeted.
7. **If you** are using Google Analytics, you can add your ID to the appropriate field.
8. **Check** the following fields: "Use Categories for META keywords," "Use Tags for META keywords," "Dynamically Generate Keywords for Posts Page," and "Autogenerate Descriptions."
9. **Click** the blue "Update Options" button at the bottom of the page.

Now that you have set up the plugin, at the bottom of the editing page for each page or post, you will see an "All in One SEO" box; you can choose specific page titles, descriptions, and keywords for each page that override the general settings you have just set up. For example, if you

have created a page that provides information on "Activities on the Normandy Coast," you should now add relevant search engine information that applies to that page only, and not the rest of the site. (If you don't input information for individual pages or posts, the default information you filled in for the home page will be applied to that page.)

NAMING AND LABELING YOUR IMAGES IN A SEARCH ENGINE-FRIENDLY WAY

It's important to name your images in a meaningful way, as this can help boost your site's position for the right keywords. Instead of keeping a string of numbers (e.g. IMG_1397.jpg) or assigning a random name to the file, before you upload it, name the image in a meaningful way that includes your main keywords—for example, "b-and-b-normandy-coast-front.jpg." Be sure to complete the "Title" and "Alternate Text" fields in the Media Library, as well (e.g. "B&B Normandy Coast, front view of the house").

TIP

Some themes, such as the "Mystile Theme," have their own SEO area. You can choose to use "All in One SEO Pack" instead, or you can configure their special SEO area. If you do the latter, I suggest inputting a custom home page description and keywords, and setting it so you can input a custom description and keywords for each page and post.

3. EXTERNAL FACTORS

You've now done what you can do to prepare your site for the search engines, as far as the site itself is concerned. But there are two other major factors that determine how your site will be ranked:

> **how much traffic it gets**

> **how many relevant inward links it has**
  (that is, other people mentioning your
  site on their website and linking to it)

How much traffic you can send to your site at the outset depends on how much traditional and word-of-mouth marketing you can do; trying to achieve inward links from other sites in the same broad area as you is also essential— it sends Google the message that your site is recognized by others, and therefore deserves a good ranking.

At the beginning, you may only have a little traffic and just a few inward links, but with consistent promotion, you will see both increase, and will be able to watch your site moving up in the rankings.

SUBMITTING YOUR SITE TO SEARCH ENGINES

The most important search engine is Google; Bing and Yahoo have a (small) part of the market share as well. Submitting your site isn't actually necessary, as the search engines' "spiders" will automatically crawl all sites that are linked to from other sites. However, you can get a head start by submitting your site from the following web addresses:

https://www.google.com/webmasters/tools/submit-url
(You will need to set up a Google Webmaster Tools account.)
http://www.bing.com/toolbox/submit-site-url
(Bing now powers Yahoo.)

Note that it may take several weeks for your site to appear in the listings, so don't worry if you don't see it listed right away (see page 150).

Integrating social media
WITH YOUR WEBSITE

"Social media" is the label given to a group of web-based "tools" that allow users to share and exchange information and ideas with a network of other users.

Social media provide fabulous communication tools for the website owner, enabling you to:
> reach more people
> remind them about you
> engage with them more fully

I'm assuming that you're already familiar, at least to some extent, with the broad concept of social media—Facebook and Twitter, for example, are regularly mentioned in the mainstream media. But even if you feel that social media really isn't your thing, I do suggest you consider it if only for website promotion purposes. This section will look at how social media can be used specifically for this and integrated into your website.

Which social media you choose to use will depend on the kind of world you're in; here we'll look at the six most-used social media, but there are others that may suit you as well (see the box on page 145 entitled "Other Social Media").

Social media & YOUR WEBSITE

Keeping in touch:
if someone "likes" or "follows" you, you can reach them again

Like

Promotion:
by "liking" or "following" you, people spread the word about you; they can also come across you accidentally, e.g. on YouTube or StumbleUpon

Repurpose your content:
if you put your website content on social media, or your social media content on your website, you can introduce your content to a different audience

FACEBOOK

In order to use Facebook as a communication tool for your website, you need to set up a business page on Facebook. You can then invite people to "like" you on your Facebook page, or better still, directly from your website. Once someone has "liked" you, your Facebook posts will appear in their news feed.

Posting on your business Facebook page is a good way of sharing small snippets of information, photographs, and short news updates you want people to be aware of.

To set up a Facebook business page, go to http://www.facebook.com and click on the link underneath the green "Sign up" button entitled: "Create a Page for a celebrity, band or business."

Integrating Facebook into your site

Display a "Like" button in your sidebar with the "Facebook Like Box" widget that comes with Jetpack (once you've activated Jetpack, you'll find it in the Appearance > Widgets area ready to drag into your sidebar). You can choose to have it with, or without, the faces of your fans.

Alternatively, you can add a simple button that links to your Facebook business page from your sidebar by using the "Social Media Icons Widget" (see page 145).

Facebook is a trademark of Facebook, Inc.

TWITTER

Twitter is used to send out and comment on short, immediate pieces of news and information that are right up to the moment. You can use this as a tool to interact with visitors and give updates on developments on your website. To create an account, go to https://twitter.com/signup and follow the instructions. People who choose to "follow" you will now be able to read your messages (known as "tweets") on their Twitter home page.

Integrating Twitter into your site

Display your latest tweets with the "Jetpack Twitter" widget (find it on your Appearance > Widgets page).

You may also want to include a "Follow" button so people can sign up to follow you without leaving your website. To do this, log into your Twitter account. Go to https://twitter.com/about/resources/buttons, select "Follow," and choose from the "Button options," then copy the code in the box.

In your website admin area, go to Appearance > Widgets and drag a "Text" widget into the sidebar. Paste the code into the widget and save it.

Note: if you want to show the number of followers you have, change "false" in the code to "true" (see the screenshot below) and save the widget. If you show the number of followers, the widget may be too wide for your sidebar —if this is the case, choose the version of the button that doesn't show the username.

As with Facebook, you can put a button that links to your Twitter page in your sidebar using the "Social Media Icons Widget" (see page 145).

REBELMOUSE

RebelMouse (http://www.rebelmouse. com) incorporates your Facebook, Twitter, Google+ (and other) posts into one "front page" that resembles a Pinterest pinboard. The RebelMouse WordPress plugin gives you a tall, thin sidebar widget perfect for the blog pages of your site, or lets you create a page that you can easily incorporate into your site.

 ## LINKEDIN

LinkedIn is mostly for professional networking, but if your site is a presentation of you and your professional skills, it may be useful to include a button on your site that will take visitors to your LinkedIn profile. To get a LinkedIn account, sign up here: http://www.linkedin.com.

Adding a LinkedIn button to your site

Log into your LinkedIn account; go to http://www.linkedin.com/profile/ profile-badges. Choose which button you want to use, and then copy the code in the box next to it. Go to your Appearance > Widgets page and drag a text widget into your sidebar. Paste in the code and save the widget. Alternatively, use the "Social Media Icons Widget" (see opposite).

YOUTUBE

We've seen how YouTube can be used to host videos so you can embed them into your site, but it can also be used as a fantastic promotion tool. Through uploading videos you've created yourself (in which you talk about your field, give a tutorial, or show your products),

you can establish yourself as an authority in your domain and gain a following of fresh new site visitors who would never have come across you otherwise. Of course, whether this is a suitable means of promoting your site will depend on what it is you do. To create a YouTube account, sign in at http://www.youtube.com with your Google account (or create one by clicking "Sign In" then "Create an account").

You can put a button that links to your YouTube channel in your sidebar using the "Social Media Icons Widget," or you can embed your videos directly into the site.

PINTEREST

Pinterest has become a huge phenomenon; if your site is artistic or creative, you will have a lot of fun creating "pinboards" of images you like and allowing users to interact with them by commenting, "liking," or "repinning" your images to their own boards. To sign up with Pinterest, either go to http://pinterest.com, or sign up for a business account at http://business. pinterest.com.

For business sites, you'll need to verify your site. Choose the option to "Verify with a meta tag." Copy the meta tag they generate for you. In the admin area of your website, go to Appearance > Editor. Looking at the right-hand side, click on the link that says "Header;" find "<header>" in the code that is displayed, and right after this, paste the code you've copied. Click "Update File." On the Pinterest site, click "Click here to complete the process" to finish.

Adding a Pinterest button to your site

Log into your Pinterest account. Go to http://pinterest.com/about/ goodies/; scroll down until you see the "'Follow Button' for Websites" heading. Choose the button you want on your site and copy the code. Back in your admin area, go to Appearance > Widgets and drag a text widget into your sidebar. Paste the code into it and save the widget. You can also use the "Social Media Icons Widget" for Pinterest; the "Social Sharing Toolkit" plugin is also very useful (see opposite), allowing you to easily add "Pin it" buttons to your pages.

 ### GOOGLE+

Whether you choose to include Google+ depends on whether you think your visitors will be using it, but along with the rest of the suite of Google tools, it's definitely here to stay.

Integrating Google+ into your site

Go to https://developers.google. com/+/plugins/badge/; fill in your Google+ web page address and choose how you'd like your button to appear. Copy the code. On your Widgets page, drag a text widget into your sidebar; paste the code into it and save the widget.

Google and the Google logo are registered trademarks of Google Inc., used with permission.

TIP

There are dozens of different ways to integrate social media into your website, and vice versa. For example, you can choose to have your blog posts display on your LinkedIn profile page, or on Facebook, etc. Look at other people's sites for ideas on integrating social media.

REVIEW SITES

Do you run a brick-and-mortar business, a restaurant, or a hotel? If so, it is worth paying attention to review networks. Simply Googling a few of your competitors will show you if people are leaving reviews about them and on which networks (for example Yelp!, OpenTable, TripAdvisor, Foursquare). You can ask your customers to leave feedback or even incentivize them to do so—although obviously, the feedback they leave is entirely up to them!

Include all your buttons in your sidebar at once

The "Social Media Icons Widget" is a useful plugin that allows you to add all your social media buttons to your sidebar simultaneously. All you need to do is install the plugin via the Plugins > Add New area, then drag the widget to your sidebar in the Appearance > Widgets area. Configure the web addresses for each of the social media you want to use by clicking on the icons, choose your style, and you're done.

The "Social Sharing Toolkit" plugin is another useful tool you may want to investigate. It's more complicated to set up, but it allows you to add Facebook "Share," Twitter "Tweet," and Pinterest "Pin it" buttons from the same interface.

Some other social media

> Delicious
> Digg
> Flickr
> Reddit
> StumbleUpon
> Instagram
> Tumblr

THE JETPACK SHARING FEATURE

The Jetpack "Sharing" feature lets you add Facebook, Twitter, LinkedIn, Pinterest, and other social media buttons right into your site pages and posts so that people can "share" them without leaving your site. From within the Settings > Sharing area, drag the services you want to use into the "Enabled Services" area; you can then choose how you want them displayed. You can also include "Email" and "Print" buttons.

Note that the plugin lets your site visitors "like" or tweet (etc.) directly from the page, but it doesn't allow them to visit your Facebook page or choose to "Follow" you on Twitter (or go to any of your other social media "home pages"). You'll need to add these buttons separately.

In the "Sharing" area, you can also see how, using the Jetpack "Publicize" feature, you can integrate your blog posts with other social media so that each time you post on your blog, your material also appears on the selected social media.

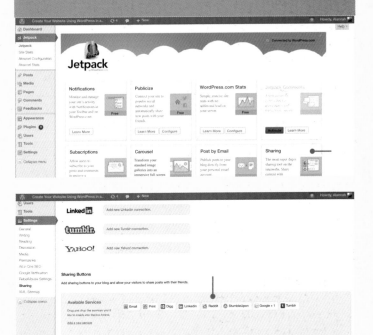

The Jetpack "Sharing" plugin.

10

Useful things to know

TROUBLESHOOTING

Legal ISSUES

You may or you may not be doing business from your website; however, there are certain rules all websites need to comply with, and you will need to make sure you are aware of these from the outset. In addition to general business regulations, take care to check out specific rulings concerning online business—as noted below.

PRIVACY POLICIES

Specific laws, depending on which state or region of the world you are in, demand that you publish a privacy policy declaring—among other elements— how you collect data from your website visitors and what you plan to do with it. Make sure you stick to these rules, as you don't want to be accused of violating the privacy of site visitors (see SBA's website: http://www.sba.gov/community/blogs/community-blogs/business-law-advisor/creating-privacy-policy-your-online-business).

COOKIES

New laws concerning cookies (text files that contain information—usually a site name and unique user ID) and other web-tracking tools have recently been enacted in the EU, so if you are doing business with any of the affected countries, you will also be liable to comply with these laws. (See this link for some useful information: http://www.ico.gov.uk/for_organisations/privacy_and_electronic_communications/the_guide/cookies.aspx)

You may think your site doesn't use cookies, but if you are using Google Analytics or running any advertising, it does—therefore, you will need to find out which laws (federal, state, and international) apply to your website or business, and make sure you include a way to obtain users' consent on your site. A simple statement may be adequate, but make sure you check out the particular recommendations that apply to where you live.

COMMERCIAL EMAIL

The US CAN-SPAM Act specifies clearly what you need to do to make sure your commercial emails keep within the law. For guidelines, see here: http://www.business.ftc.gov/documents/bus61-can-spam-act-compliance-guide-business. Similar, though not identical, laws apply in the UK and the different EU countries.

The SBA website (http://www.sba.gov) is a good place to find out about business, federal, and state law and regulations for U.S. citizens or residents.

TIP

A number of WordPress plugins, such as "Cookie Law Info," exist that allow your users to agree to the use of cookies on your site.

TIP

If you are in any doubt about any of these matters, seek professional help from a qualified individual or a relevant local advisory. If based in the U.S., visit the U.S. Small Business Administration's (SBA) website, www.sba.gov, for up-to-the-minute legal advice, and links to relevant federal and state organizations.

Huge fines have been imposed on companies violating data protection, so make sure your site complies with these regulations.

The CAN-SPAM Compliance Guide details how to make sure your commercial emails stay within the law (http://www.business.ftc.gov/documents/bus61-can-spam-act-compliance-guide-business).

BUSINESS PERMITS AND OTHER LEGAL REQUIREMENTS

If you are doing business from your website, you need to research all of the legal requirements relevant to your type of business—you may also need a business license and permit to work from home. Take note that as well as varying from country to country, these rules can also be different from state to state. If you are doing business with other countries, you will also need to ensure you adhere to international trade laws (for more information, visit: http://www.hg.org/trade.html).

TRADEMARKS AND COPYRIGHT

If you want to safeguard your brand or your material, make sure you implement the necessary measures beforehand so you don't find your carefully built-up brand, images, words, or even products have been "borrowed" by someone else. As shown by numerous stories of people whose online identities have been usurped by others because adequate precautions weren't in place, it really pays to research this properly. You also want to make quite sure that you aren't treading on someone else's toes, before you begin. (For more information on trademark and copyright laws as these relate to the internet, see: http://www.internetlegal.com/trademark-law-and-the-internetcopyright-law-and-the-internet/)

EU Data Protection and Freedom of Information advice—EU privacy laws are overseen in the U.K. by the Information Commissioner's Office.

SOME USEFUL PLACES TO GO FOR INFORMATION:

Federal Trade Commission
http://www.ftc.gov
PCI Security Standards Council
https://www.pcisecuritystandards.org
Bureau of Consumer Protection (CAN-SPAM Act)
http://business.ftc.gov/documents/bus61-can-spam-act-compliance-guide-business
United States Copyright Office (copyrighting online works)
http://copyright.gov/circs/circ66.pdf
ICO (European Cookie Law)
http://www.ico.gov.uk/for_organisations/privacy_and_electronic_communications/the_guide/cookies.aspx
ICO (Data Protection)
http://www.ico.gov.uk/for_organisations/data_protection.aspx

Maintaining your WORDPRESS SITE

UPDATING WORDPRESS

WordPress is constantly being tweaked and improved, so it makes sense to keep your installation up to date, both to make the most of these improvements and to ensure your site remains secure.

When a new version of WordPress is released, you'll see a notification at the top of your administration area. All you need to do is click the "Please update now" link and then click the blue "Update now" button. You don't need to reinstall anything, and it only takes a few seconds. But what you must do before you update is make a backup of your site just in case anything goes wrong—see "Backing up" below.

In the same way, when a plugin or a theme requires updating, you'll see a notice on your screen—you can update from within the admin area, without having to reinstall.

Make sure you back things up first, and allow time to test everything afterward, whenever you perform an update.

BACKING UP

Making a backup of your site means keeping a copy of it in case something goes wrong. How often you choose to back up your site depends on how often you update it, but you should schedule regular backups, and keep several copies of these (for example, on a DVD or on DropBox*, as well as on your computer).

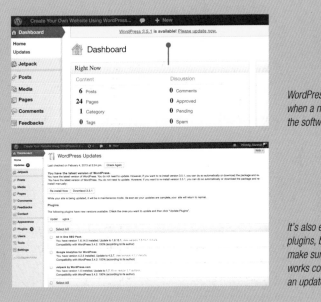

WordPress notifies you when a new version of the software is available.

It's also easy to update plugins, but you need to make sure everything works correctly after an update.

DropBox (http://www.dropbox.com) is a very useful way of storing digital material—photos, documents, and videos—online.

The backup takes place in two stages:
> backup of your site files
> backup of your database

Of course, this can be done manually using FTP software and by logging into the database area of your hosting administration, but the easiest way is by using a plugin such as BackUpWordPress, which backs up both of these for you automatically.

Using BackUpWordPress

1. Install the plugin as usual by going to Plugins > Add New and searching "BackUpWordPress." Install and activate the plugin.

2. Go to Tools > Backups; click "Settings." Schedule the plugin to back up both the database and your site files, and decide how frequently you want it to perform the backup. Put your email address in the "Email notification" field and click "Update."

3. Once the backup has run, you will receive the zip file by email if it is small enough, otherwise click the download link in the email you've been sent, or make a copy of the backup by clicking the download link in your "Backups" area. (The system will also store the backups in your hosting system.)

My site isn't showing up in GOOGLE

Did you submit your site via Google Webmaster Tools, at https://www.google.com/webmasters/tools/submit-url? Google can take a few weeks to list sites, so it's possible that its spiders simply haven't had the chance to crawl to it yet. (Spiders are programs that crawl the web for keywords that enable users to find what they are looking for.)

Are there any other sites that link to yours? This is an absolutely essential first step for the marketing and search engine visibility of your site. You can be sure that if you have any links inwards to your site, Google will find it.

You can do two things to ensure Google spiders crawl all the pages of your site: request a crawl via Google Webmaster Tools and/or add a sitemap to your website.

To request a crawl:
1. **Log in** to your "Webmaster Tools" account.
2. **Add** the site to your account.
3. **Verify** the site using the "Google Site Verification" plugin.
4. **Inside** your "Webmaster Tools" account, click the web address of your website.
5. **Click** "Health" on the left-hand side, then "Fetch as Google."
6. **Type** the web address that you want Google to crawl, leaving "Web" selected from the drop-down; then click "Fetch."
7. **When** you see "Success" under "Fetch Status," click "Submit to Index;" then choose the "URL and all linked pages" button, and click "OK."

To add a sitemap to your site:
1. **Add** the "Google XML Sitemaps" plugin to your site.
2. **Under** Settings > XML Sitemap, click the link where you see "The sitemap wasn't built yet. Click here to build it the first time" (as in the screenshot below). That's all you have to do—the major search engines will be automatically notified each time you make a change to your site.

TIP

If your site isn't showing up in Google, do check that you don't have the checkbox next to "Discourage search engines from indexing this site" selected (in Settings > Reading).

Building a sitemap using the Google XML Sitemaps plugin.

Working with OTHER USERS

If you're working as a team, you can assign other users a "role"—that is, access with varying rights, depending on what you want them to do. Either assign the other users a role from within the "Users" area, or allow them to sign up by providing a signup box using the "Meta" sidebar widget. (The default new-user role can be set in the "General Settings" area; you can alter the individual user's role once they have signed up.)

ROLES ARE:

Administrator
The person who has access to all the administration features (you).

Editor
A user who can publish and manage posts and pages, as well as manage other users' posts.

Author
A user who can publish and manage their own posts.

Contributor
A user who can write and manage their posts, but not actually make them live (someone with editor rights can do this).

Subscriber
A user who can only manage their profile.

If you need to have several blogs on one domain, or different blogs on multiple sub-domains, you can make use of the "Multisite" feature, which is now an integral part of WordPress. This is a fairly complex matter—see here for more details: http://codex. wordpress.org/Create_A_Network

Getting HELP

If you're ever stuck, here are two places you can go to get help.

The first is the "Help" button at the top right of the screen; this gives you relevant information on the area of administration you are currently in.
The second is WordPress.org.
A very useful "Frequently Asked Questions" area may provide all the information you need (http://codex.wordpress.org/FAQ); also try the forums (http://wordpress.org/support)—you can post your problem and receive a timely answer, but see relevant posts first as it's likely someone has already experienced the same problem, so the answer may be there.

The "Help" button at the top of each screen gives you help for the particular area of the admin you are in.

WordPress in other LANGUAGES

It's easy to install WordPress in a language other than English—at the time of writing, the "core" WordPress instalment exists in 74 different language versions. This will mean that as long as you are using a relatively uncomplicated theme, all the text that appears automatically on the website—dates, and so on—as well as the admin area, will be in your selected language.

INSTALLING WORDPRESS IN ANOTHER LANGUAGE

Unless you are using a local hosting company that offers a one-click installment of WordPress in your own language, you'll need to install your language version of WordPress manually. To install manually, you will need to create a MySQL database from your hosting package's control panel, and you'll also need to be able to upload to your website ("FTP")—you can usually do this directly from your control panel.

To create a database, and accessing your files via FTP, in Dreamhost:
In Dreamhost, go to Goodies > MySQL. Click the link at the top of the page entitled "MySQL documentation in our wiki!" and follow the instructions to create a MySQL database. To access your site files via FTP, go to Manage Domains > Web_FTP (a link underneath your domain name); a new window will open up which may take a moment to load. When loaded, type ftp. yourdomain.com next to "host", log in using the FTP username and

password you were assigned when you signed up, and click the green tick. Click on "yourdomain.com"—you can now see all your site files and folders listed inside.

To install WordPress in your own language:
Go to http://codex.wordpress.org/ WordPress_in_Your_Language. On this page there are links to instructions for installation in many different languages; simply follow the instructions in your language.

If there aren't any specific instructions available for your language, you'll need to install WordPress in English (you can use the one-click install) and then change the language over to your own. For this, you'll need to access your site files via FTP (as mentioned, this can normally be done via your hosting control panel). When you've completed your install, switch the language by following the instructions here: http://codex. wordpress.org/Installing_WordPress _in_Your_Language (see the sections "Manually Installing Language Files" and "Single Site Installations").

Things become more complicated when you want to use a fancier, premium theme. These usually contain words and phrases that belong to the theme, that are not part of the basic installation of WordPress. These need to be translated, and in most cases, it will have to be you who does the translation.

There are guidelines that programmers need to follow to ensure a theme will be translatable. However, because WordPress is a free software with thousands of individuals creating themes for it, no one obliges the programmers to consider their global audience. If a theme has been designed along these guidelines, you will be able to translate it into your own language, following the instructions detailed here.

TIP

When a theme is described as "translation-ready," it means you can apply the translation process. Sometimes this isn't specified, so it's a good idea to check with theme creator. It's also worth asking if there are any language files for the theme already in existence, for the language you require; some themes do have versions in other languages, and the creators will happily let you have them. Occasionally, themes have a built-in area in the theme options that allows you to translate words and phrases very easily.

TRANSLATING A THEME

The translation process is most simply done by using a free plugin called Codestyling Localization.

1. **Install** and activate the plugin in the normal way via your admin area.
2. **Go** to Tools > Localization.
3. **Click** "Themes" and identify the theme you are using from the list of themes.

4. **Click** "Add new language" and select the language from the window that pops up; click the "create po-file" button.
5. **Click** "Rescan," then click "scan now" in the window, allow the files to scan, and click "Finish." (In the screenshots, I am about to carry out a translation into French.)
6. **Now** click "Edit," next to the "Rescan" button.
7. **Translate** all the words and phrases that appear on the live part of the website (next to each word or phrase to be translated, click "Edit" and then save the translation). You do not need to translate the words and phrases that belong to the admin area (unless you want to translate this as well).
8. **When** you're done, click "generate mo-file."
9. **Go** to your live site, refresh the page, and check how it looks.

For the free Structure theme (p.114), you need to carry out an extra step to translate the theme to your own language. After you have completed steps 1-6 above, navigate to your FTP or file manager area from within your hosting company control panel. (In Dreamhost, go to Manage Domains > Web_FTP (underneath your domain name); type ftp.yourdomain.com next to "host" in the window that opens, and log in using the FTP username and password you were assigned when you signed up. Click the green tick). Go to yourdomain.com > wp-content > themes > organic_structure_free_v3-1 and move the two files you have created (which will look something like "fr_FR.mo" and "fr_FR.po") to the directory titled "languages." And you're done.

For further information on using the plugin, see: http://www.code-styling.de/english/development/wordpress-plugin-codestyling-localization-en. You can also translate plugins using the Codestyling Localization plugin.

Multilingual sites

For sites that need to be in multiple languages, there are several solutions:
> Create separate directories and install and set up WordPress in each of them; create a "custom menu" with links to each to allow users to choose their language.
> Use a plugin such as qTranslate that allows you to create all pages and posts in multiple languages; a sidebar widget allows the site visitor to select their language from a dropdown menu.
> Use WMPL, an extremely popular premium plugin (http://wpml.org/; you'll need the "Multilingual CMS" version).

Adding functionality with PLUGINS

You will find plugins that can do all manner of things listed in the WordPress Plugin Directory—see here: http://wordpress.org/extend/plugins

Remember, you can install them directly via the Plugins > Add New area of the admin—just search their name.

Plugins mentioned in the book:
> Akismet
> Jetpack
> Pixeline's Email Protector
> All in One SEO Pack
> WooCommerce
> WooDojo
> AWeber Web Form Plugin,
  MailChimp List Subscribe Form
> Subscribe2
> Google Analytics for WordPress
> Social Media Icons Widget
> Cookie Law Info
> BackUpWordPress
> Google Site Verification
> Google XML Sitemaps
> Codestyling Localization—for translating themes
  and plugins
> Q-translate, WPLM (premium)—for multilingual websites

MORE PLUGINS
The following are a selection of plugins you may find useful to extend your site's functionality, but there are many more to investigate . . .

underConstruction—a really useful plugin for when you're building your site, or performing maintenance, and you don't want visitors to see what you're doing.
WPtouch, WP Mobile Detector—automatically transform your site to a mobile theme when viewed on a mobile.
Shareaholic—nice-looking social media sharing buttons, including the often-seen "sexy bookmarks" and "classic bookmarks" options.
Contact Form 7, Really Simple CAPTCHA—a contact form for your site (an alternative to the Jetpack one.

Add a CAPTCHA to it (a letter/number code) to protect your contact form from submissions by robots.
Events Manager, Event Registration—online event management and registration.
MapPress Easy Google Maps—add Google Maps with custom markers to your site.
Membership, Wishlist Membership (premium)—create a membership site.
Link Manager, Link Library—organise your links, create a links directory.
Ad Squares Widget—allows you to display the grid of 125 x 125 pixel adverts very often seen on websites; it's also compatible with Google AdSense.*
Google AdSense Plugin—allows you to display AdSense* ads as a widget.
Yet Another Related Posts Plugin—lets your blog readers see a list of related posts they may also be interested in; also useful for bringing your archived material to the fore.
NextGEN Gallery—a hugely popular plugin that helps you to upload and maintain image galleries.
Slideshow (by StefanBoonstra)—an easy-to-use plugin that allows you to set up a slideshow anywhere within a page or a post or even as a sidebar widget.

Google AdSense is an ad network that displays ads on your website that are relevant to your page content. You receive revenue according to the number of clicks generated from your web pages.

Going further with WORDPRESS

WordPress is a fantastically flexible software that can be made to do just about anything—that's why books covering it in detail are encyclopedic in scope and size. This book is intended to go as far as you possibly can in just a weekend to get your initial website up and running, and to help you plan your ongoing marketing strategy, but there is much more you can do with WordPress:

> create a network of blogs or sites
> run a social network or community portal
> set up a forum
> create a membership site
> manage events
> build a directory
> start a classifieds site
> build a review site
> create a media-sharing website
> set up a fundraising site

WordPress is so well supported, and has so many designers and programmers creating themes and plugins for it all over the world, that whatever it is that you wish to do with your website, there is probably a WordPress theme or plugin already in existence that will enable you to do it.

If you need a developer to create something for you, here are some places you can find one:
Code Poet Directory *http://directory.codepoet.com*
WPMU Jobs *http://premium.wpmudev.org/wpmu-jobs*
Smashing Jobs *http://jobs.smashingmagazine.com*
WP Hired *http://www.wphired.com*
ThemeForest *http://themeforest.net*
(you can contact the developers directly)
Elance *https://www.elance.com*
Freelancer.com *http://www.freelancer.com*
ODesk *http://www.odesk.com*

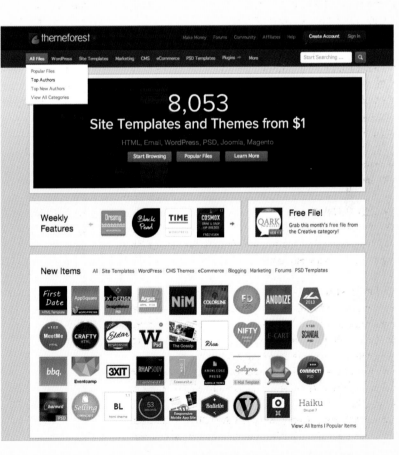

You can search for Top Authors on ThemeForest to find a suitable developer.

Resources

Domain registration
http://www.namecheap.com
http://www.godaddy.com
http://www.gandi.net

Places to get ideas for domain names
http://www.instantdomainsearch.com
http://www.domainsbot.com
http://www.namestation.com
http://www.nameboy.com
http://domai.nr
http://www.dotomator.com

Check who owns a domain
http://www.betterwhois.com

Hosting companies
http://www.dreamhost.com
http://www.bluehost.com
http://mediatemple.net
http://www.hostgator.com
http://www.webhostingpad.com

Stock images
http://www.istockphoto.com
http://www.fotolia.com
http://www.shutterstock.com
http://www.clipart.com

Image editing software
http://pixlr.com
http://www.gimp.org

Logo creation
http://buildabrand.com
http://99designs.com

Background images
http://www.patterncooler.com
http://www.colourlovers.com
http://www.backgroundlabs.com
http://subtlepatterns.com

Video and other elements that can be embedded in your WordPress site
http://www.youtube.com
http://vimeo.com
http://www.dailymotion.com
http://www.viddler.com
http://qik.com
http://blip.tv
http://www.hulu.com
http://www.flickr.com
http://instagram.com
http://photobucket.com
http://www.smugmug.com
https://soundcloud.com

http://polldaddy.com
http://revision3.com
http://www.scribd.com
http://www.slideshare.net/
https://twitter.com

Taking payment online
http://www.paypal.com
http://www.google.com/wallet/

Themes
http://wordpress.org/extend/themes/ (free)
http://wordpressthemesbase.com (free)
http://www.wpdaddy.com (free)
http://www.s5themes.com (free)
http://www.freewpthemes.net (free)
http://www.wpskins.org (free)
http://wptemplates.org (free)
http://wpshower.com (some free)
http://www.dessign.net (some free)
http://shakenandstirredweb.com (some free)
http://templatic.com(some free)
http://www.skinpress.com (some free)
http://wordpress.org/extend/themes/ commercial (premium)
http://www.studiopress.com (premium)
http://themeforest.net (premium)
http://www.elegantthemes.com (premium)
http://www.woothemes.com (premium)
http://ithemes.com (premium)
http://templatic.com (premium)
http://press75.com (premium)
http://www.organicthemes.com (premium)
http://www.mojo-themes.com (premium)
http://themetrust.com (premium)
http://thethemefoundry.com (premium)
http://graphpaperpress.com (premium)
http://www.obox-design.com (premium)
http://www.wpzoom.com (premium)
http://www.wpnow.com (premium)
http://www.frogsthemes.com (premium)
http://www.theme-junkie.com (premium)
http://www.templatelite.com (premium)

Advertising
http://adwords.google.com

Email marketing/newsletters
http://www.aweber.com
http://mailchimp.com
http://www.constantcontact.com
https://www.icontact.com
http://www.campaignmonitor.com
http://www.benchmarkemail.com
http://www.pinpointe.com
http://www.getresponse.com
http://www.verticalresponse.com

Tracking
http://www.google.com/analytics/

Search engine submission
https://www.google.com/webmasters/tools/submit-url/ (submit site)
http://www.bing.com/toolbox/submit-site-url (submit site)
https://www.google.com/webmasters/tools/ (Google Webmaster Tools, to verify with Google and request site crawl)

Social media
http://www.facebook.com
https://twitter.com
http://www.linkedin.com
https://plus.google.com
http://pinterest.com
http://www.flickr.com
https://www.rebelmouse.com

Review sites
http://www.yelp.com
http://www.opentable.com
http://www.tripadvisor.com
https://foursquare.com

Places to find developers
Code Poet Directory
http://directory.codepoet.com
WPMU Jobs
http://premium.wpmudev.org/wpmu-jobs
Smashing Jobs
http://jobs.smashingmagazine.com
WP Hired http://www.wphired.com
Themeforest http://themeforest.net
(you can contact the developers directly)
Elance https://www.elance.com
Freelancer.com http://www.freelancer.com
ODesk http://www.odesk.com

WordPress
http://wordpress.com (the version of WordPress that is hosted for you)
http://wordpress.org (the home of self-hosted WordPress)
http://codex.wordpress.org/FAQ (Frequently Asked Questions)
http://wordpress.org/support/ (support forums)
http://wordpress.org/extend/themes/ (free themes directory)
http://wordpress.org/extend/plugins/ (plugin directory)
http://codex.wordpress.org/WordPress_in_Your_Language (foreign language versions of WordPress)

Glossary

http://codex.wordpress.org/Installing_WordPress_in_Your_Language (changing your WordPress installation from English to another language)

Online storage
http://www.dropbox.com

Demo sites
http://wordpresswalkthrough.wordpress.com (WordPress.com demo site)
http://www.createyourwebsiteinaweekend.com/twentytwelve (default theme demo site)
http://www.createyourwebsiteinaweekend.com/responsive/ (Responsive Theme demo site, example of a free business theme)
http://www.createyourwebsiteinaweekend.com/visual/ (Visual Theme demo site, example of a free portfolio theme)
http://www.createyourwebsiteinaweekend.com/structure/ (Structure Theme demo site, example of a free magazine theme)
http://www.createyourwebsiteinaweekend.com/mystile/ (Mystile Theme demo site, example of a free e-commerce theme powered by the free e-commerce plugin WooCommerce)

YOUR ADMIN AREA
http://www.yourdomain.com/wp-admin—access to the admin area of your own self-hosted WordPress site (replace www.yourdomain.com with your own domain name)

COMPANION WEBSITE
http://www.createyourwebsiteinaweekend.com—see here for updates, demos, tips, and latest information; join the newsletter to keep informed.

Admin(istration) area This is the "behind the scenes" area of your website where you set up how it will look and input your content; your site visitors will never see this part. (It is also sometimes known as the "back end," whereas the public part is referred to as the "front end.")

Avatar A graphic representation of a user or the administrator (you) each time a comment is posted on a site. If you set up a "Gravatar"—a globally recognized avatar linked to your email address—the image you choose will be shown on your site (or anywhere else you might post). Set up a gravatar here: https://en.gravatar.com

Backup A copy of your site that you keep in a safe place (or several safe places) in case anything goes wrong with your site. You can use a plugin to make backups regularly (see Chapter 10).

Blog A section of your site (or a standalone site in its own right) consisting of dated posts ordered chronologically, with the latest first. These are usually fairly short, newsy items relating to one person or one topic or interest and they usually aim to attract interaction or reader comments.

Browser (or "internet browser") The software (such as Internet Explorer, Google Chrome, Firefox, or Safari) that you use to surf the Internet.

Categories These are a way of "filing" your blog posts so that if you want to, you can order them into different groups according to their subject matter. Distinct from tags (see "Tags").

CMS Stands for "Content Management System;" this means a website that the owner can log into and make changes to, without having to delve into the coding. (WordPress is a CMS.)

Comments Running a blog on your site is usually an invitation to readers to add their own remarks about what you have written in your blog post. With a WordPress site, you can choose to allow visitors to leave messages on your blog posts and the other pages on your site.

Dashboard The "home page" of your administration area.

Default theme This is the template that is automatically installed when you set up WordPress yourself (as opposed to using WordPress.com). The current default theme is called "Twenty Twelve" (as used in Chapter 5 for the model website setup).

Domain The main address of your website, for example www.yourdomain.com. Domain names need to be registered so that they belong to you for a specific period of time.

Footer The area at the bottom of a web page; usually contains copyright information but sometimes other elements as well (such as widgets).

Front end This is the public part of your website that your visitors will see.

FTP This means putting something up onto a website. This can be done either with special FTP software, or through the control panel of your hosting company's website. As you are using WordPress, you can upload things like pictures into cyberspace via its administration area, and will not have to use any separate FTP software. However, if you are installing a foreign-language version of WordPress, you will need to have FTP access to your website.

Harvest Illegally obtain email addresses for spamming purposes (see "Spam").

Header The large rectangular image often found at the top of a website. This space is often filled by a slider (see "Slider").

Hexadecimal ("hex") color A six-figure or letter code used to identify colors used on websites, usually preceded by a hash tag; for example #FFFFFF indicates white. (Sometimes colors are identified with just three figures or letters.)

Hosting This is the space that you "rent" in cyberspace where your website will be lodged.

HTML This is the basic code used to write websites (stands for Hyper Text Markup Language). If you're using WordPress, you won't need to know any of this code.

Key word or key phrase See "Search Engine."

Menu A list of links, or web page titles, that can be clicked on to navigate around a site. The menu often runs along the top of a website, but sometimes down the side, or on occasion, both.

Navigation Another name for a menu.

Page As distinct from a post. These are static pages on a website. Blog pages, on the other hand, are filled with blog posts, and their content changes when a new blog post is added.

Permalink The website address of each page and post on your site; WordPress will generate these website addresses the way you tell it to (as explained in Chapter 5).

Pingback A notification you receive to let you know that someone has linked to some of your website content.

Plugin An element you can add to your website to make it do something that it didn't originally do. For example, you can add an event management plugin to your website to display events on a calendar and allow your visitors to sign up to attend them. A vast number of free and paid-for plugins exist, designed by individual programmers or companies, which you can use to make your site do virtually anything you want it to.

Post A blog post is a dated article that will appear at the top of the blog section of your site. A blogging site will usually choose to display blog posts on the front page; however most other types of site will have a blog section somewhere inside the site.

Robot Also known as a "bot," "crawler," or "spider"—a program that "crawls" (visits) websites in order to index information for the search engines.

RSS This is a "feed"—or stream of content—that readers can use to read in a "Feed Reader" if they are an avid blog-follower. Many will choose instead to receive your blog updates by email, which you can allow them to do via the Jetpack plugin (see Chapter 5).

Search engine When you are looking for something on the Internet, you will use a search engine, such as Google, to find it; the search engine you are using

will return a list of sites it considers relevant to what you are looking for. (The word or phrase you type into the box to make your search is known as a "key word" or a "key phrase.")

Self-hosted This is the form of WordPress that you install yourself on your own hosting space. As distinct from sites running with WordPress.com, you have total control over your website (see Chapter 1 for a comparison).

SEO Stands for "Search Engine Optimisation." This means doing the best that you can to ensure that your site has the highest possible position in the search engines, in order to be visited by the maximum number of people (see Chapter 9).

Sidebar This is the (optional) column on the right or the left hand side of your website pages, which is usually used to display widgets (see "Widgets").

Slider A large, rectangular space at the top of your home page, in which a number of images, sometimes with captions, and occasionally videos, rotate. These are often linked to pages inside the site or to blog posts.

Social media Services, such as Facebook and Twitter (see Chapter 9), that allow users to share and comment on information, photos, and videos with a network of other users.

Spam Commercial email that you have not asked for—in other words, junk email. We also refer to comment spam, which is caused by promotional messages submitted, usually by robots, as comments on your website. Luckily, these can mostly be filtered out using the Akismet plugin (see Chapter 5).

Subscribe A site visitor can choose to "subscribe"—i.e., receive your blog posts or website updates by email or through a "Feed Reader;" we also talk about newsletter subscribers who are people who have "opted in" (chosen) to receive your email newsletters.

Tags You can attach tags (key words) to your blog posts, which is distinct from assigning them to categories; tags are primarily used to help your site visitors find related material.

(Categories are used for filing, whereas tags are about ideas and associations.)

Theme A template that is applied to a WordPress site. Every WordPress site needs a theme; WordPress will be installed with the default theme, and it is up to you whether or not you choose an alternative. It controls the colors, fonts, and everything to do with the look of the site; some themes also determine the layout—for instance, the theme may determine that you have a slider on your home page with a row of three boxes underneath it. Some themes are free, whereas others you have to pay for (these are referred to as "premium" themes).

Trackback Another type of notification you receive to let you know that someone has linked to something on your website.

Traffic People visiting your website.

Tweet A short snippet of information posted on the social media network Twitter is known as a "tweet" (see Chapter 9).

Upload To put something up in cyberspace or up on your website. With WordPress, you will upload images to your Media Library through your admin area.

URL Means simply a website address. It can be the home page, or a page somewhere else on a website. (Stands for "Uniform Resource Locator".)

User Someone signed up with a WordPress website. There are five levels of user, each of which has different rights; some can create pages and other content, others can just read posts (see Chapter 10).

Widget An element—usually situated in the sidebar, sometimes in the footer area of a site—such as a search box, a list of recent posts, a small text announcement, or a list of recent "tweets."

WordPress.com This is the easy option for running a WordPress website; sites hosted on this system are very simple to set up, but your options are limited (see Chapter 1).

Index

Acknowledgments

Thank you to my clients and workshop partipants for inspiring me to write this book. Thank you to my editors (Ellie Wilson, Nick Jones, and Zara Larcombe of Ilex Press) for their endless patience, good sense, and sanity. Thank you to WordPress for creating such a wonderful system, and to all the theme authors and website owners who've allowed me to print their beautiful creations in these pages. Thank you to my friends for bearing with me, and for all the encouragement and enthusiasm I've been met with along the way.